D1690926

FIVE TYPES OF
LEARNING

Timeless Wisdom and Recent Research

CAROLE BOGUE, Ph.D.

iUniverse

FIVE TYPES OF LEARNING
TIMELESS WISDOM AND RECENT RESEARCH

Copyright © 2018 Carole Bogue, Ph.D.

All rights reserved. No part of this book may be used or reproduced by any means, graphic, electronic, or mechanical, including photocopying, recording, taping or by any information storage retrieval system without the written permission of the author except in the case of brief quotations embodied in critical articles and reviews.

iUniverse books may be ordered through booksellers or by contacting:

iUniverse
1663 Liberty Drive
Bloomington, IN 47403
www.iuniverse.com
1-800-Authors (1-800-288-4677)

Because of the dynamic nature of the Internet, any web addresses or links contained in this book may have changed since publication and may no longer be valid. The views expressed in this work are solely those of the author and do not necessarily reflect the views of the publisher, and the publisher hereby disclaims any responsibility for them.

Any people depicted in stock imagery provided by Getty Images are models, and such images are being used for illustrative purposes only.
Certain stock imagery © Getty Images.

ISBN: 978-1-5320-4133-4 (sc)
ISBN: 978-1-5320-4132-7 (e)

Library of Congress Control Number: 2018901954

Print information available on the last page.

iUniverse rev. date: 03/232018

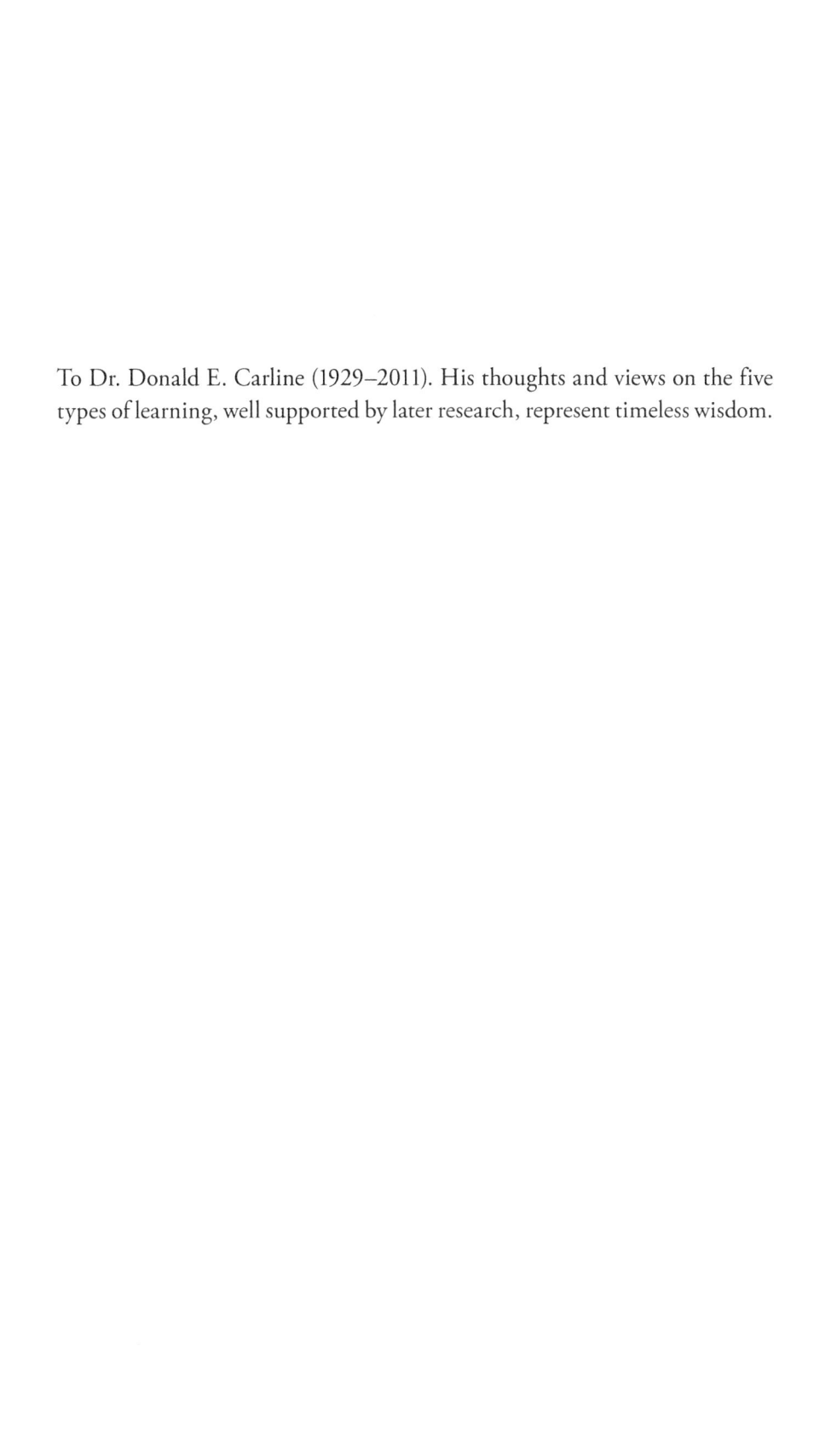

To Dr. Donald E. Carline (1929–2011). His thoughts and views on the five types of learning, well supported by later research, represent timeless wisdom.

CONTENTS

Preface xi
Acknowledgments xxi
Introduction xxiii

Part 1—Sensory Experience Learning: Timeless Wisdom 1
    Introduction 2
    Words Not Substitutes for Percepts... 2
    The Development of Percepts and Their Importance 5
    Percepts Not Yet Formed 5
    Recalled or Reconstructed Percepts 7
    Determining Needs 9
    Feeling Need 9
    Reality-Based Percepts 10
    Percept Apparatuses 10
    Self-Activity 11
    Function of Sensory Aids 12
    Application Exercises 13

Part 1—Sensory Experience Learning: In Light of Recent Research 15
    Introduction 16
    Some Definitions 16
    Sensory Processing 17
    Patterns of Sensory Processing 18
    Classroom Structure 19
    Classroom Application 20
    Visual and Auditory Perception 20
    Auditory Processing 24

Phonological Processing and Phonological and
Phonemic Awareness 24
Implications for the Classroom 26
Sensory Experience Learning and a Multisensory Learning
Environment 27
References for Part 1—Sensory Experience Learning 28

Part 2—Memory-Type Learning: Timeless Wisdom 33
Introduction 34
Background Needed for Memorization 34
Pupils' Observations and Positions Named: 36
Maximum Use of Background Possibilities 37
Responses with Strong Background Possibilities 37
Responses with Weak Background Possibilities 38
Activities Following Development of a Background 39
Application Exercises 42

Part 2—Memory-Type Learning: In Light of Recent Research 43
Introduction 44
Multistore Models 44
Working Memory Model 45
Information Processing Models 46
How Children's Brains Memorize Facts 49
Enhancing Learning and Memory—
Based on Brain-Based Research 50
References for Part 2—Memory-Type Learning 58

Part 3—Motor-Type Learning: Timeless Wisdom 61
Introduction 62
Steps in the Acquisition of a Skill 62
Application Exercises 68

Part 3—Motor-Type Learning: In Light of Recent Research 69
Introduction 70
Definition 70
Classroom Application 72
Strategies to Develop Motor Skill 72
Whole versus Part Instruction 74
References for Part 3—Motor-Type Learning 75

Part 4—Problem-Solving-Type Learning: Timeless Wisdom 77
    Introduction 78
    Importance of Reasoning.. 78
    Types of Reasoning... 79
    Reasoning and Nonreasoning Activities 81
    Opportunities in Teaching to Promote Reasoning.............. 83
    Environment for Instilling a Love of Reading, Learning, and
    Reasoning... 83
    Practical Guidelines for Teaching Children to Think........ 87
    Development of Personal Attributes: A Real Value 89
    Application Exercises... 90

Part 4—Problem-Solving-Type Learning:
        In Light of Recent Research................................. 93
    Introduction 94
    Definition.. 94
    Focus on Background Knowledge and Intelligence........... 95
    Dispositions Involved in Critical Thinking 97
    Common Core State Standards and Critical Thinking..... 99
    Need for Direct Instruction.. 101
    Instructional Strategies: Schema-Based
    Problem-Solving Strategies 104
    Other Instructional Strategies/Techniques...................... 106
    References for Part 4—Problem-Solving-Type Learning................... 111

Part 5—Emotional-Type Learning: Timeless Wisdom 117
    Introduction 118
    Conduct Attributes—Learning to Live and
    How to Make a Living... 120
    Appreciation Attributes—Learning to Live 121
    The Development of Attributes 121
    Stages in Development of Attributes................................ 124
    Ideal Environment for Attribute Development 129
    Application Exercises 133

Part 5—Emotional-Type Learning: In Light of Recent Research 135
    Introduction 136
    Early Work 136

Social and Emotional Learning (SEL) 137
Keys to Implementation... 138
Common Core State Standards 139
Preparation for the Workplace 140
Collaborative for Academic, Social, and
Emotional Learning (CASEL) 141
References for Part 5—Emotional-Type Learning 142

PREFACE

It is an honor to communicate the philosophy and thoughts about the five types of learning that were captured in a document that somehow has been long lost and forgotten. The information conveyed, however, is very powerful and most applicable to today's classroom environment. It needs to be shared with teachers and parents everywhere.

In the early to mid-'70s, a group of graduate students at the University of Colorado–Boulder benefitted significantly from the sage tutelage of Dr. Don E. Carline. I was one of those students, but I didn't realize at the time that he had sorted out the key aspects of the learning process and applied the important principles and approaches that he recommended for the K-12 educational program in university classrooms. While completing doctorate degrees, all of us grew in significant ways because of this multitalented leader and educator, perhaps one of the most charismatic and engaging individuals the world would ever know, whose death occurred on January 16, 2011. As many of his graduate students commented, he was "larger than life," and people like him tend to live on through others—those they've touched—for generations to come.

Our impression of Dr. Carline was largely created by his approach to helping students, preparing lectures, writing and implementing grants, and reaching life's goals. A man of genuine enthusiasm and a creative thinker, he was dedicated to helping others around him and did so in significant ways. He not only carefully prepared for his classes and monitored grants, spending hours on end in his office, but as an ardent program adviser, he reached out to his graduate students frequently with the goal of facilitating their program completion. He often asked about the students' progress in course work and reviewed dissertation ideas laboriously. When students neared program completion, he helped them find employment; indeed, he wrote numerous letters of recommendation while facilitating job searches.

Dr. Carline also intuitively understood that to persist with the doctoral program, students needed to achieve a modicum of balance in their lives. In fact, he often inquired if students were spending sufficient time with their families, as most of the students were thoroughly dedicated to their studies. He asked about their families and made it a point to meet as many family members as possible, expressing a strong current of unquestionable interest and support.

As an educator at the university, he went far beyond the classroom and reached out locally, regionally, and on a statewide and national basis. Through his grants, he assisted the Colorado K–12 schools and counseled them in helping students succeed. He took his graduate students with him to the school sites so they could observe his approach to providing guidance to the schools, their teachers, and their administrators. On one visit to an elementary school in Pueblo, Colorado, in which I participated, it was obvious that subsequent to his guidance, the teachers led their students to significantly higher performance levels. Those teachers had nothing but praise and admiration for him and thanked him profusely for his assistance. That evening he treated all of the students who visited the school site to a movie, *The Sting*, starring Paul Newman and Robert Redford. Through such excursions, he provided graduate students not only the opportunity to directly observe application of learning principles in the classroom but also a chance to discuss any course or program concerns. Gifted with small talk, he made such visits enjoyable, interesting, and engaging. In so many ways, he was earnestly thoughtful.

And then there were the annual Boulder Reading Conferences every summer. At the conclusion of the conference, the tradition was to present awards to many in attendance as a way to recognize their participation and contribution to the sessions. In the summer of 1973, my second experience at these conferences, it was my task to introduce Dr. Carline, who would announce the winners and grant the awards. I did so as follows, clearly illustrating the admiration that my fellow doctoral candidates and I had for this insightful, personable, and inspirational educator, leader, and adviser:

Ode to the Great

The epitome of

    charm
    benevolence
    alacrity
    humanism
    brilliance
    integrity
    determination
    and efficiency

One who makes everyone feel "great"
    when in his presence
Truly, the greatest of all
    our beloved
    our leader
One responsible for such a rewarding conference
None other than Dr. Carline

> Thank you, Dr. Carline! We are so grateful to you for this most informative and useful conference.

I then presented a small gift to him on behalf of those in attendance. And for all these years, I have saved this introduction that I had typed on onion-skin paper and filed with his document/manuscript that you soon will read.

While at the university in the roles of professor and adviser, he also served as president of the International Reading Association for two years and earned national recognition for his work at the university and in the state of Colorado. Many educators across the country reached out to him and sought his counsel and advice.

Not only did he work zealously to help his students and others already in the field of education, but his approach to life and classroom instruction was filled with enthusiasm and energy. Further, he had a passion for baseball, which he played professionally in earlier years, racquetball, and football. I don't think he ever missed a Colorado home football game, where Ralphie, a live buffalo mascot of the University of Colorado Buffaloes, entertained the fans before each half of the games. Dr. Carline's zest for life extended to supporting his family, his beautiful wife and daughters, who often visited him in his office and endeared themselves to all of us. I recall thinking that I should emulate him and his approach to work and life, but as mentioned, he was larger than life, and I doubt that any of us have enriched the lives of so many.

I can truly say that he was instrumental in providing me the opportunity to successfully navigate a career in education, and for that I am forever grateful. After completing the PhD program, I worked with K–12 students on an individual basis and with countless small and large groups of college students who demonstrated deficient skills in reading, writing, and mathematics. In order to effectively assist these students, I drew upon my knowledge of the five types of learning to create instructional programs that would help students increase performance levels in essential skills and improve application or transfer of these skills to textbook material. In order to facilitate skill transfer or application, I wrote several books in various content areas for student use. When conducting instruction and using my books in formal learning environments, I witnessed a significant increase in student skill levels and improved application of skills to content areas. To this day, I draw upon my knowledge of the five types of learning when assisting students in the learning process.

If Dr. Carline were writing this preface, he would emphasize that his thoughts were gleaned over many years of reading, study, and application in the classroom. His desire to narrow discussion about learning to a few basic principles, illustrated through storytelling, was driven by the goal to succinctly describe key understandings that we, as educators and parents, should know and apply. When I learned of his passing a few years ago, I felt such deep remorse and regret because I had planned on visiting him and his family the following summer. I also learned that he had never pursued publishing his material that addressed those key understandings, although he had shared his material with his graduate students. I knew that I had a copy of his work somewhere in my files, and with some searching, I found this remarkable document and began reading it again so many years later. I was convinced that his thoughts needed to be shared with others. His ideas about the learning process and the keys to facilitating learning resonated with me when I reviewed his material. As I reread various portions, I saw that his words of wisdom, shared in a marvelous storytelling manner, were most applicable to today's schools and would have a far-reaching impact on student learning. It was apparent, however, that a thorough review of the literature was warranted in order to determine if and how current research supports his ideas.

In conducting the review, I read hundreds of articles and books, and, as expected, I found significant support for his description of each of the five types of learning and how to facilitate them. This book presents his description of each of the five types in the "Timeless Wisdom" sections. Each of these sections is followed by my summary of recent studies and analyses in the "In Light of Recent Research" sections. I included the essence of his material in the "Timeless Wisdom" sections, although I did edit the material.

It is important to point out as well that each of the "Timeless Wisdom" sections concludes with an "Application Exercises" subsection. These subsections, drawn from Dr. Carline's material, provide thought-provoking questions and discussion items related to the type of learning just presented. The items are designed to generate deliberation about the types of learning, so these subsections can be used effectively in professional workshops and other group settings, as well as in college classrooms.

This book, then, consists of five major parts, each of which presents Dr. Carline's description of a type of learning, followed by my discussion of that type of learning in light of recent research. Below is a brief summary of each of the five parts.

"Part 1—Sensory Experience Learning: Timeless Wisdom" addresses the development of percepts through hearing, seeing, tasting, smelling, touching, and handling the content of the environment. Percepts of sight, sound, growth, motion, and position, as well as kinesthetic, taste, and smell percepts that are required in many learning situations are discussed. Emphasis is placed on the need for learners to have the percepts in order to comprehend the words used to express ideas and on the need for teachers to foster students' recall of helpful percepts and to build background when necessary through sensory experience learning.

"Part 1—Sensory Experience Learning: In Light of Recent Research" focuses on research that addresses the principles presented and the requirement to design multisensory learning environments that are based on the needs of students, including each child's pattern of sensory processing, and on an understanding of sensory integration. It is stressed in this section that such environments need to reflect results of research focused on perceptual learning and perception, patterns of sensory processing, and visual and auditory perception and processing, including phonological and phonemic awareness and phonological processing.

"Part 2—Memory-Type Learning: Timeless Wisdom" describes prompt mental responses and examines the activities that facilitate these responses. Emphasis is placed on the need for teachers to build a background of meaning, especially for material with significant and related ideas. This kind of content typically implies associations that rely on a background of understanding. Even for material with weak background-building possibilities, teachers are encouraged to provide some background or suggestions and lead discussion of percepts in order to facilitate memorization. Further, the reader is reminded that some material may not need to be memorized.

Activities discussed that facilitate memorization include (1) guiding students to practice recall during the process of memorization, (2) providing true-to-use activities or meaning for words/content to be memorized, and (3) addressing organization of material to be memorized, either as a whole or in parts, depending on the content.

It is noted that memorizing to recall prompt or relatively prompt mental responses is an important and often-used method for learning and for demonstrating what one has learned. Teachers are urged to conduct student activities that provide strong background so that the content can be reduced to prompt responses and can "take root, grow, and hold fast."

"Part 2—Memory-Type Learning: In Light of Recent Research" reviews memory theory, including information processing models and strategies to enhance learning and memory. Sensory memory, working/short-term memory, and long-term memory are described. Emphasis is placed on enhancing memory, and definitions for metacognition, metamemory, and metacomprehension are provided. The importance of paying attention, including establishing a purpose for learning, previewing material to be learned, and marking material effectively, is addressed. Further, certain strategies for activating prior knowledge and experience, facilitating active involvement, constructing meaning, and facilitating ability to retain information and demonstrate learning are discussed, as well as the importance of distribution of practice. The necessity for understanding individual learning needs when applying pedagogical strategies to enhance memory is underscored.

"Part 3—Motor-Type Learning: Timeless Wisdom" discusses motor skills, or skills that require coordination of the brain, nervous system, and muscles and involve actions that demand muscle movement. Gross and fine motor skills are differentiated, with focus placed on what is required to develop motor skills, including a mind-set and clear percept of the skills, accurate initial performance, and, in some cases, practice for speed of execution. Also addressed are a few related principles for directing motor learning: learning the skill in parts or as a whole; using true-to-life conditions for addressing the correct initial performance and conducting practice; and determining the length of practice periods and distribution of practice over a period of time.

"Part 3—Motor-Type Learning: In Light of Recent Research" defines motor skills and focuses on the steps essential to learning these skills and on some instructional strategies that facilitate their acquisition, such as demonstrating and discussing the skill, providing assistance to students who are learning a motor skill based on their prior experience with that skill, and sharing prompt feedback during initial and repeated attempts in order to ensure correct skill development from the start. Further, the need for teachers to assist students in establishing goals in order to motivate student repetition is discussed. This section also addresses whole versus partial instruction for the best learning of motor skills.

"Part 4—Problem-Solving-Type Learning: Timeless Wisdom" addresses the importance of reasoning, inductive and deductive reasoning, and the need for "maximum individual effort." Focus is placed on strategies for leading students to develop reasoning skills, including posing appropriate questions, remaining alert to opportunities for developing problem-solving skills, establishing learning goals for students, and determining the kind of material/content to use. Further, emphasis is placed on the need to adapt the problems assigned to a student's capacity, interest, and experience. A description of the Uninterrupted Sustained Silent Reading process is provided. Also included are practical guidelines for teaching children to think and a discussion of the importance of growth in personal attributes, fostered by problem-solving opportunities, as an aim in school learning.

"Part 4—Problem-Solving-Type Learning: In Light of Recent Research" defines problem solving / critical thinking and focuses on the need for background knowledge and reliance on "dispositions," or habits, such as attitudes or habits of mind and other essential aspects of critical thinking. Also addressed is the inclusion of critical thinking in the Common Core State Standards and the need for direct instruction in critical thinking in today's schools. Instructional strategies mentioned include schema-based strategies/ interventions for mathematical problem solving, activities designed to lead students to transfer critical-thinking skills across various knowledge domains, provision of "advance organizers" and generative-learning activities, as well as strategies, including cooperative-learning methods, use of open-ended problem types, activities and assessment tasks using real-world problems, classroom assessment techniques, the case-study method, and inquiry-based approaches. The need for teachers and teacher-preparation programs to stress the value of promoting critical thinking and problem solving in the schools using established standards is emphasized.

"Part 5—Emotional-Type Learning: Timeless Wisdom" presents the importance of leading students to develop personal attributes that influence their conduct, including tolerance, punctuality, self-control and politeness, and appreciation attributes that influence selection of hobbies and leisure-time activities in areas such as poetry, literature, art, music, the sciences, and history. How the development of personal attributes differs from other learning objectives is discussed, as well as how development of personal attributes is least understood and inherently difficult to teach. Stages in the development of attitudes are presented, and the ideal school environment for their development and provision for students' active participation are described. The need for maximum inner transformation is stressed.

"Part 5—Emotional-Type Learning: In Light of Recent Research" affirms an educational agenda that includes enhancing students' social-emotional competence, character, health, and civic engagement. Focus is placed on social and emotional learning, or SEL, that involves acquiring skills to recognize and manage emotion, set and achieve positive goals, appreciate the perspectives of others, and develop other skills necessary for success, not only in the academic setting but in the workplace and in life in general. SEL's impact on reduction of conduct and behavioral problems and on increased academic success is discussed. Keys to implementing SEL are presented, and the integration of social-emotional learning in the Common Core State Standards and the positive impact of SEL on workplace preparation and development of citizenship skills are described.

The reader will see how recent research clearly supports the thinking of this man who was so far ahead of his time. Indeed, what you will read herein can be described as the timeless wisdom of a truly enigmatic educator.

Finally, on behalf of Dr. Carline, I would like to thank his lovely wife and two beautiful daughters for their understanding and patience. While raising a family, he shared a significant amount of his time, tutelage, and support-providing assistance to his graduate students, who left the university with PhDs in hand and with little less than idolatry for this truly admirable person. Further, I must thank his wife and daughters for concurring with my goal to prepare this book to include his thoughts and *timeless wisdom*.

ACKNOWLEDGMENTS

I owe a debt of gratitude to my collaborators in preparing this manuscript for publication. First, I want to thank Allye Hobson-Robinson, who offered thoughtful suggestions, editorial expertise, and support throughout the process. Allye's contributions to the overall organization and treatment of the topics were significant.

I also would like to thank Dr. Robert Garcia, who carefully reviewed the original manuscript and provided many useful suggestions for shaping the content of this book. His recommendation to speak to all teachers working with students of various ethnic backgrounds and inspire them to follow the principles presented helped increase the value of this book for today's schools and home-learning environments.

Finally, I would like to acknowledge the helpful input, candid feedback, and never-ending encouragement of David West, MD, FACC, who supported this effort from the beginning to its conclusion.

INTRODUCTION

Teachers need to understand the learning processes that underlie the development of academic skills and acquisition of knowledge in order to effectively facilitate learning in their classrooms. What types of learning are involved? How can a greater understanding of those types of learning help teachers identify activities that lead to effective skill development and increased knowledge?

Carline noted that in order to facilitate learning, teachers will find it useful, in addition to reading relevant articles and books and taking courses that focus on learning, to conduct a personal analysis of their own learning processes as young children. They might examine specific skills that they developed or areas of knowledge that they increased. For example, they may recall learning how to sing, to play a musical instrument, to paint a landscape, to write an essay, to speak a foreign language, to solve quadratic equations, to determine the volume of a cylinder, to coach football, to put aside prejudices in weighing the soundness of new proposals, to best describe the major events of a specific war, and/or to summarize the beliefs and values of the early settlers. After listing ten or more of these skills and/or areas of knowledge, teachers would benefit from a careful analysis of the activities in which they were engaged while learning the skills and/or gaining the knowledge. Reflecting on their own learning processes, even inefficient ones, helps teachers acquire a deeper understanding of how learning occurs. If teachers used inefficient procedures to learn skills and acquire knowledge, their ability to teach others could be compromised; however, examining their own learning and reviewing the literature addressing psychologically sound principles of learning will help teachers identify effective procedures.

Careful thought and time for this analysis are required, as much is involved when choosing activities to facilitate learning. In very few instances is only one type of learning involved, and for each type, numerous activities are required. Readers need to understand the nature of the five types of learning and their related components. Consider the following brief summary:

Types of Learning and Key Factors

Sensory Experience—Sensory experience relies on the physical senses. Percepts such as size, color, shape, sound, taste, temperature, appearance, length, width, hardness, softness, texture, composition, and dimension are involved.

Memory—Memory refers to a recollection of something earlier or from the past. Memory involves prompt mental responses, such as names, dates, facts, and formulas, as well as concepts, rules, laws, and principles involving networks of connected ideas.

Motor—Motor skills involve motions carried out through the use of the muscles. Motor skills refer to skills ranging from writing to singing, dancing, swimming, operating machinery, throwing a baseball, and threading a needle.

Problem Solving—Problem solving requires concepts and skills for determining cause and effect, reasoning, analyzing relationships, making inferences and drawing conclusions, making generalizations, and applying solutions to new problems.

Emotional Learning—Emotional learning refers to understanding and effectively managing emotions. Social and emotional competencies include self-awareness and the skills, attitudes, and values involved in the process of establishing and maintaining personal goals and relationships.

These five types of learning are examined in the five parts of this book. Collectively, they contribute to the learning process that teachers need to understand when creating environments that are conducive to learning. This book will help teachers create those environments and will enable parents as well to gain an increased understanding of the types of learning when facilitating learning in a home environment.

In each of the five parts of the book, Dr. Don E. Carline's thoughts and timeless wisdom, as expressed in his earlier material, are presented. After discussion of each type of learning, I provide a summary of recent research focused on that area of learning. In preparing these summaries, I reviewed a significant body of literature. It will become apparent to the reader that results of recent studies strongly support Carline's philosophy and suggestions for implementation in today's classrooms.

PART 1

SENSORY EXPERIENCE LEARNING: TIMELESS WISDOM

Introduction

Some writers refer to sensory experience type of learning as perceptual learning. According to dictionary definitions, percepts can be viewed as impressions of things perceived through the senses that serve as the basis for concept development. Sensory experience learning involves hearing, seeing, tasting, smelling, and touching and handling the content of the environment. The products resulting from things perceived by the senses are called percepts, or the objects of perception.

Practically all knowledge is connected in some way to the world of persons and objects. In early life, children begin to recognize their parents and caretakers, their smiles and voices, the spoon, the bed, the milk bottle, the red ball, and dozens and dozens of other objects and qualities. As a child grows, sensory learning expands, and the child's learning experiences become more complex. A child gains information about numerous items, including plants, animals, persons, places, minerals, machines, instruments, sounds, colors, weights, dimensions, forms, motions, tastes, and odors. Even a child's notions of honesty, cleanliness, kindness, and politeness are associated with someone in the child's environment, and even the most complex learning depends upon sensory experiences. Through the microscope, the bacteriologist learns to recognize germs; through the telescope, the astronomer learns about planets and stars. The botanist must learn to know plants, the biologist must study cells and organs, the chemist must distinguish one element or compound from another, and the entomologist must differentiate among thousands of insects. Surely sensory experience plays a vital part in the development of knowledge and ideas.

Words Not Substitutes for Percepts

Not long ago I visited a mathematics class in which pupils were studying the metric system of measurement. The pupils had been and were memorizing facts: 1 meter = 39.37 inches; 1 liter = 1,000 cubic centimeters; 1,000 meters = 1 kilometer; 10 centimeters = 1 decimeter; 1,000 grams = 1 kilogram; and so forth. They were changing meters to centimeters or kilometers, grams to kilograms, cubic centimeters to liters, miles to kilometers, and pounds to grams. Around the room there were no yardsticks, metersticks, gram weights, quart measures, or liter measures. There was not one concrete presentation of a single measure. In fact, there was not even a representation of one in a picture or sketch. I asked the teacher for permission to ask the pupils a few questions, and the teacher gladly consented. I then asked six of the pupils, selected at random, to go to the chalkboard in the front of the room and draw a line one centimeter long. In response to this stimulus, six lines were drawn, with lengths ranging from about one inch to three feet. The majority of the lines were about one foot long or more. I then asked six different pupils to go to the board and draw a line one meter long. With this stimulus, six more lines were drawn, ranging from less than an inch to about four feet. The majority of the lines were about one foot long.

Following this activity, I asked the class to judge the number of grams in a lead pencil about four inches long. Some of the pupils, being critical, insisted on handling the pencil before venturing answers. The answers varied from one to three thousand. In response to my final request, which was to name something one kilometer from them, pupils mentioned the teacher's desk, the flagpole in front of the building, the shopping center (four blocks away), and the city of Denver, approximately thirty miles away.

These pupils' learning was bereft of percepts because of their total lack of sensory experience with the metric system of measurement. Have pupils really and profitably learned if they are able to spell a-p-p-l-e and pronounce the word but are unable to distinguish an apple from a golf ball or a watermelon? Have they really and profitably learned the meaning of a centimeter if they are unable to tell whether or not it is about the length of a city block or the thickness of a lead pencil? Learning in school can be meaningless if it is not connected with realities and meaningful percepts. Words! Words! Words! We demand that surgeons accurately know the nerves, the arteries, the muscles, the organs, and the structures before they are allowed to operate. In gaining this knowledge, sensory experience learning plays a vital role. A surgeon's learning would be lamentably incomplete, even dangerous, without it. Yet in so much schoolwork, the sensory experience type of learning is ignored, resulting in purely memorized symbols without meaning or precision supporting them. Indeed, real learning starts with sensory experience. Words cannot be divorced from the realities they represent. If words and reality are separated, the pupils grope, stumble, and fall in utter dismay, regardless of the effort expended.

Long ago, Gates and colleagues (1942), writing in *Educational Psychology*, showed the direct relationship between the meaning of words and firsthand experiences as follows:

> Learning activities in the early stages of reading illustrate the process of developing word meanings by using verbal symbols in connection with actual experiences, and later using words to represent these experiences. The background for reading is often an excursion, let us say, to the grocery store, a zoo, or a boat or marina. As the children explore, the teacher watches what the clerks, animals, or sailors do and actually performs some of the operations, being careful to use words that characterize these experiences. The pupils are encouraged to use the same words—to verbalize their experiences while they are enjoying them.
>
> Back in the classroom, the children and the teacher discuss their recent experiences. They use the words they heard and spoke "on location." But now the concrete situation is absent. The words fulfill a representative function—they signify what the children saw and heard and did on the excursion. As the discussion proceeds, the teacher may write on the board a series of sentences describing the children's experiences. These descriptions become the content of a *meaningful* reading project. What meanings become clear when the pupils read these statements? Just what do the symbols stand for—their experiences in the store, or the zoo, or the boat? In a very real sense, they do not get meaning *from* the printed materials but *take meaning to it*.
>
> This illustration suggests a fundamental general principle: Words mean only what they represent in our experience. Poverty of ideas is therefore associated with meagerness of contact with the world of things and persons. (428–429)
>
> Years later, in descriptions of elementary reading programs, this concept is referred to as the "language experience"

approach. Such an approach has been highly recommended for the classroom.

The Development of Percepts and Their Importance

In teaching children, the first prerequisite is to determine carefully the part that percepts play in whatever is to be learned. One can say that the words used to express ideas cannot go beyond the percepts that the learner has of these word-expressed ideas. The learner must have the percepts in order to comprehend the words. If the learner does not have the percepts, the teacher needs to provide appropriate experiences that will lead the learner to develop them. In the example of pupils studying the metric system, the pupils were without percepts; therefore, they knew little or nothing about the metric system. They were memorizing word symbols without percepts of these symbols. In teaching, it is imperative to ensure that pupils have appropriate percepts before proceeding with the lesson. *Whenever the experiential background of pupils is insufficient for them to proceed with understanding, the teacher needs to help them build a background through sensory experience learning.*

There are actually two situations in which the experiential background is inadequate: (1) when the percept needed has never been developed or formed and (2) when a percept already developed and formed is not used in the interpretation of a new learning situation.

Percepts Not Yet Formed

In the first situation, the experiential background has never been acquired, but percepts should be developed at the very beginning to provide a foundation for what follows. Several examples below depict the importance of developing percepts early when striving to teach toward certain learning goals or objectives.

- ❐ Many learning situations demand *visual* percepts of size, form, and structure of objects. Our case of the metric system is a good example. Because the pupils never had experienced the metric system, their background was deficient and called for initial strengthening by means of perceptual material. In some instances, percepts are gained through experiences with real things. In other cases, they are formed through representations of real things, but formed they must be. When learning about plants, animals, various forms of mechanics, art, and arithmetic, pupils need to acquire innumerable percepts of genuine objects. Many teachers talk about weeds, flowers, trees, grains, and insects without making any effort to lead children in developing visual percepts of them. Such omission occurs in an environment bountifully teaming with live content.

There is the classic illustration of the child attending a school located on the bank of the Missouri River, who, when asked in class to tell what the little line on the map was, answered, "The Missouri River." Then, when asked if he had ever seen the Missouri River, the child replied, "No."

There is also the story of the sixth-grade boy who studied lumber measurement but had never seen a board foot. Further, many children over the years have memorized poetry without having the faintest percept of the objects, persons, or situations at the center of the poems. What a reminder in these stories for teachers everywhere! Whenever the children's perceptual background is insufficient to enable them to visualize what is being studied, a teacher must add meaning and reality to their background by providing sensory experiences.

- ❐ A second example of when pupils have not formed percepts involves learning that requires percepts of *sound*. Pronunciation of words is derived chiefly through percepts of sound. Many teachers have placed too little emphasis on the potency of sound in the learning environment, yet correct sound percepts are often indispensable if progress is to be made. Also, children from homes in which English is a second language may accept the wrong sounds as genuine, so the mistakes in grammar that they make are actually the result of incorrect sound percepts that are deeply ingrained in their home environment and/or area where they live.
- ❐ Another example of when pupils need an enriched experiential background involves learning that requires percepts of *growth* and *motion*. In a recent teaching situation that I observed, pupils found

it almost impossible to gain a working knowledge of a gasoline lawnmower engine without basing the information on the study of a real lawnmower engine—not only the engine at rest but the engine in motion as well. Pupils need similar sensory experience to understand all machines and instruments, such as those that run by steam, those that run by electricity, the gears in a car, sewing machines and others. Further, many of our skills, such as dancing, swimming, walking, and riding, are supported by motion percepts.

❐ A child who writes small *a*'s by beginning at the right and going left (reversal of what should be done) has the incorrect motion percept. Experiments have shown that motion percepts too immense for classroom presentation by the teacher, such as processes involved in farming, are efficiently shared through films. Pupils develop growth percepts, in contrast to motion percepts, through a series of observations extending over a period of time, while development is taking place in some part of the environment singled out for study, such as the life history of moths, flies, grasshoppers, and butterflies; or the growth of flowers, grains, and plants; or long and continuous transformations of any kind. If films are used to show these transformations, the stages of development can be shown in more rapid succession than in natural transformations.

❐ *Position* percepts are important also in the content of school learning. Social studies, geography, and history, for example, require location of rivers, cities, mountains, and special topological features.

❐ Pupils develop *kinesthetic* percepts, which involve both muscular and touch experiences, in learning to judge, for example, the texture of cloth or the stiffness of matter.

❐ *Taste* and *smell* percepts are truly ingrained within the individual and often go hand in hand. These percepts contribute to the understanding of numerous topics in school content.

Recalled or Reconstructed Percepts

Many interpretations, bordering upon the abstract, can be initiated and promoted when pupils use percepts already formed or quickly develop them by reconstructing past experiences. Children may overlook using percepts as interpretive aids in new learning situations, but—and for this reason—the teacher must foster the recall of helpful percepts in meeting new, complex learning situations.

To understand the use of percepts already formed in order to interpret new situations, consider the science adage: It is hard for an empty bag to stand upright. While attempting to explain this adage, pupils tend to refer to a previous experience with bags and use the percepts of sugar, flour, or potato bags in their explanation. They often say that the bag collapses when the sugar or flour is taken out, but, of course, the explanation is purely material and not the one intended by the adage. Pupils do have percepts that will help them understand the correct meaning, provided the percepts are recalled and somewhat reconstructed, but the pupils may not link the percepts with the new situation. In such instances, the teacher needs to promote the recall of appropriate percepts, either from the real or from the children's reconstructed experiences.

Now suppose two boys are depicted. One boy comes from a home where the father and mother are honest. The parents have taught the boy to be honest as he grows up in an honest living environment. The other boy comes from a home where the father and mother are dishonest. The parents tell their son to take things he needs, but to do it so that others will not see him, and the son grows up to live dishonestly. One day temptation comes to both boys. Each boy, walking along in a different part of the city, sees a woman lose a five-dollar bill. Which one of the boys will be a really honest person in this situation? Why? From this vantage point, it is easy for children to conclude that the boy full of honesty will stand firm and upright in time of temptation and stress, while the boy with no honesty will be empty and collapse morally. Who will win a mile race? Who will resist disease? Who will commit crime? Who will accept a bribe? The answers to these questions give broad meaning to the adage. In every case, however, percepts of personal human relationships initiate and promote understanding.

In directing learning, then, teachers should clearly understand the part that percepts play, and if they find or foresee that the learners' experiential backgrounds are insufficient, they must build up the learners' backgrounds through sensory experience learning. Also, teachers must lead learners to recall percepts already formed when meeting and interpreting new situations.

Determining Needs

Although teachers may understand the importance of percepts and how sensory experiences help shape them, they need further information in order to efficiently direct sensory experience learning. One guiding principle to consider is that teachers must identify percept-forming activities that are based on apparent pedagogical needs. In their scheduling of such activities, teachers should not be influenced by trends or popularity of a certain activity. Instead, they should focus on the needs of the learners when designing quality instruction and the percept-forming activities.

In a certain elementary school, the teacher shows films on a weekly basis to a sixth-grade science class. While the films may lead students to develop percepts, the content often is unrelated to the topics currently discussed in the science class. The films come on schedule, however, and they are shown on the same day every week, requiring the pupils in the science class to give 20 percent of their schooltime mechanically and regularly to view these films.

In another school, the teacher organizes field trips, excursions of various kinds, and visits to industries and other installations to help pupils develop percepts related to the topics discussed in class. The pupils definitely benefit from these activities, as they are based on pedagogical need. In addition, these percept-forming activities are incorporated at the proper time in the instructional program, as designated learning goals and outcomes are met. A trip to the museum proves valuable when pupils seek percepts needed for deeper understandings about a specific topic. A visit to the same museum proves less profitable when it is undertaken merely for the sake of going somewhere. In all sensory experience learning, we must remember: *Use activities for sensory experience learning when there is a pedagogical need for them.*

Feeling Need

Another important factor in directing sensory experience learning is preparing children so they are ready and able to form percepts. Preparing students to form percepts involves stimulating or building their need to know about a topic and then developing related percepts. For example, a teacher could lead students to develop a need to know about silk and how it is secured and manufactured. The teacher might first ask questions such as, "Where do we get silk?" and "How do we make silk so that its colors are sufficiently vibrant for use in scarves and other items?" In leading students to develop a need to learn about this topic with such questions, teachers prepare students to form percepts. Teachers then conduct percept-forming activities. Doing so may involve placing relevant information on the chalkboard or assigning certain library reference materials that, in this case, illustrate the manufacture of silk.

In fact, when children listen to a teacher discuss a topic that is difficult to comprehend, children welcome an example or illustration. At times, they may speak up in class and request concrete illustrations. They may say, "What exactly do you mean by role-playing?" A good teacher not only develops the need to know about a topic but also schedules percept-forming activities to meet that need.

Reality-Based Percepts

Teachers should provide percept-forming opportunities that are as closely associated with reality as possible. The little line on a map is not at all the same as the real Missouri River. Looking at a picture of a lawnmower engine is entirely different from viewing and examining a real lawnmower engine. The textbook drawing of a butterfly is not the genuine butterfly. The textbook description of the operation of a farm is far different from what can be depicted in film. Whenever possible, teachers should use real and genuine objects and experiences to help students develop true-to-life percepts.

Percept Apparatuses

Elaborate and expensive percept-forming apparatuses and equipment for presenting material may not be needed, generally speaking, nor are they always the most effective. Probably in the great majority of cases, common and inexpensive percept-forming materials, obtained or devised by the teacher, can prove most effective and expedient. Sketches, drawings, maps, and graphs on the chalkboard; examples of instruments, apparatuses, and pieces of mechanical and electrical equipment; weeds, flowers, grains, and a host of materials from the plant and animal kingdom in the immediate environment; stories, examples, illustrations, and analogies from the teacher's experience and knowledge—and many others near at hand—are effective and inexpensive for producing vital percepts. A small cotton gin made from a small box, a spindle, some nails, and a few wires may provide, with the aid of a little imagination, a true picture of the workings of a cotton gin, and the percept developed may be better than one developed through a very expensive apparatus. The environment is full of genuine percept-forming objects. It is a frailty of human nature to look out into the far faraway, while the "acres of diamonds" lie at our feet.

Self-Activity

Paramount in sensory experience learning should be the notion of pedagogically sound self-activity. In a certain social studies program, children submitted to the teacher beautiful maps of the United States. The oceans and lakes were colored a sea blue, the rivers were included, and the mountains were skillfully depicted in their proper locations. Some important cities were represented by almost perfect stars, and the printing was indeed remarkably well done. How happy the teacher was to show the work of her youngsters to the principal!

Not being entirely convinced, the principal asked if he might take her class for a few minutes. He sent the pupils to the chalkboard and asked each of them to draw, without help from anyone, a map of the United Sates and to show and label the important bodies of water, the rivers, the mountains, and the cities. What a sorrowful showing these youngsters made! The Mississippi River was flowing into the Missouri River, oceans exchanged places, states were labeled incorrectly, Chicago was on the Gulf of Mexico, Texas was smaller than the surrounding states, and great changes and upheavals occurred everywhere. One would not think that the land of the free could change so much! What the teacher thought was real learning proved to be more thoughtless copying with no trace of accurate percepts behind it. The teacher did not realize that pupils must actively engage in forming percepts. In this case, the activity demanded of the pupils was not pedagogically sound.

Often sensory experience learning is ineffective because the pupils are passive; they are never held for a real test of their learning. At other times, children have no opportunity to manipulate or investigate, or they have little or no time to internalize the percepts.

A teacher of migrant children in a small rural Colorado town suggested individual conferences with children so that they might explain and demonstrate the operation of a lawnmower engine by actually manipulating and describing the operational working order of the machine and even labeling some of the parts. Before school, after school, during lunch period, and during recess, children were found studying and manipulating the parts of the lawnmower engine.

There is a difference between naming ten weeds and identifying ten weeds displayed before students on a board. The former is memorization of symbols, but the latter is a test of percepts formed. There is a difference between drawing a map of the United States with its rivers and cities and mountains, using a textbook map as a guide, and sketching that map with only percepts to guide or lean upon.

Enough has been said to share this fundamental strategy: *Set the stage in sensory experience learning so that pupils are not passive but genuinely active, using well-developed percepts.* Passivity leads to fleeting percepts; genuine self-activity leads to real and lasting impressions.

Function of Sensory Aids

Recently, the use of sensory aids has expanded tremendously, especially in education. Schools have placed too much emphasis upon the written or spoken words as a medium of learning while not placing enough focus on real or representative items. All sensory aids are truly materials of instruction. They are a means to an end. Films, tapes, slides, field trips, excursions, and many other forms of contact with reality serve to guide learning. They should not be viewed as externals or extras. Sensory experience learning includes use of sensory aids of all kinds. Good teachers, who also are good "educational psychologists," sense the best time to facilitate learning through use of sensory experiences, including audio-visual aids. The advent of learning stations and listening centers has done much to increase facilitation of sensory learning. It is not necessary, then, to provide rules and schedules for offering instruction through sensory aids. The teacher who understands the crucial importance of sensory learning will know the way. Handling it in any other manner would be creating a mumpsimus.

Application Exercises

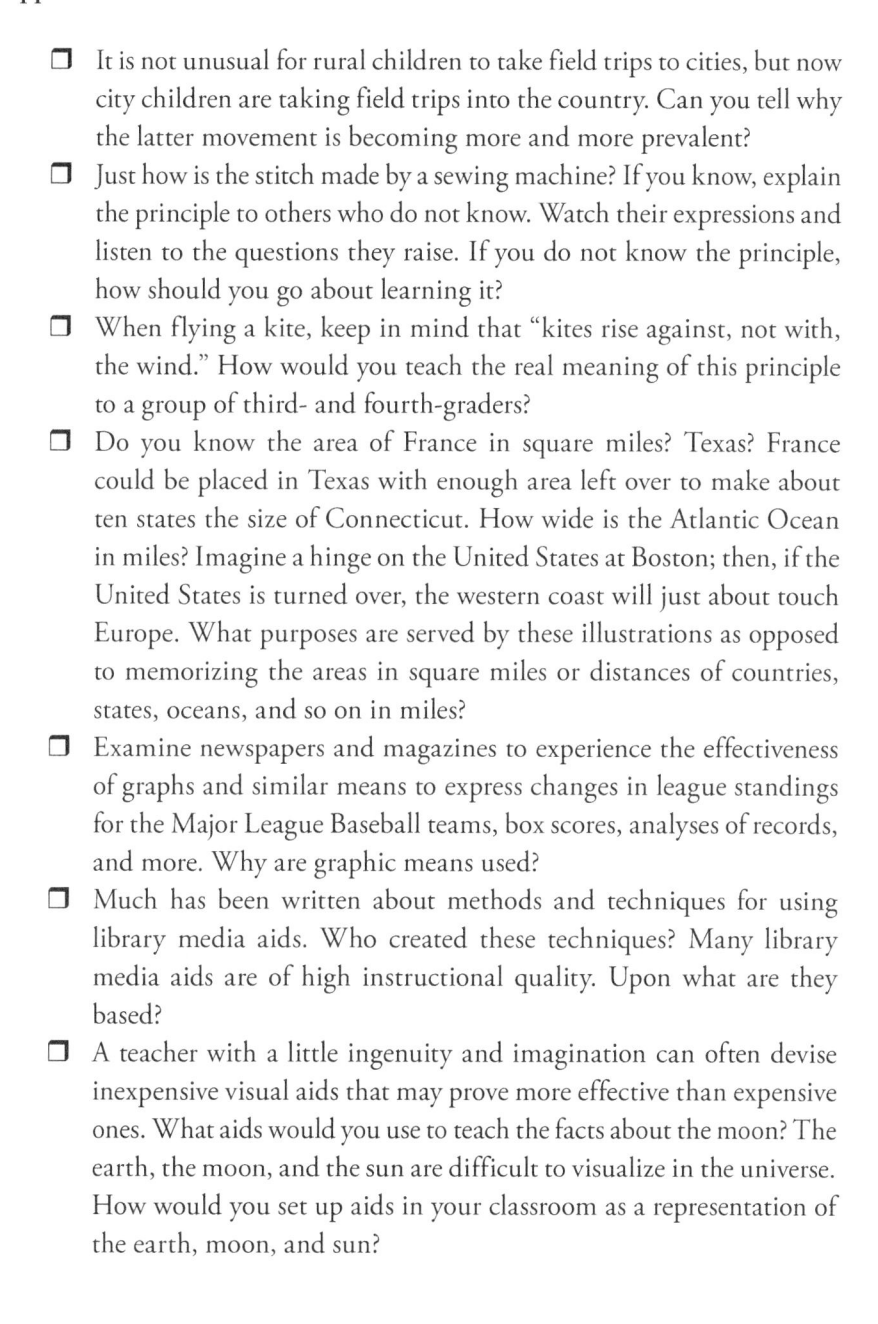

- ❒ It is not unusual for rural children to take field trips to cities, but now city children are taking field trips into the country. Can you tell why the latter movement is becoming more and more prevalent?
- ❒ Just how is the stitch made by a sewing machine? If you know, explain the principle to others who do not know. Watch their expressions and listen to the questions they raise. If you do not know the principle, how should you go about learning it?
- ❒ When flying a kite, keep in mind that "kites rise against, not with, the wind." How would you teach the real meaning of this principle to a group of third- and fourth-graders?
- ❒ Do you know the area of France in square miles? Texas? France could be placed in Texas with enough area left over to make about ten states the size of Connecticut. How wide is the Atlantic Ocean in miles? Imagine a hinge on the United States at Boston; then, if the United States is turned over, the western coast will just about touch Europe. What purposes are served by these illustrations as opposed to memorizing the areas in square miles or distances of countries, states, oceans, and so on in miles?
- ❒ Examine newspapers and magazines to experience the effectiveness of graphs and similar means to express changes in league standings for the Major League Baseball teams, box scores, analyses of records, and more. Why are graphic means used?
- ❒ Much has been written about methods and techniques for using library media aids. Who created these techniques? Many library media aids are of high instructional quality. Upon what are they based?
- ❒ A teacher with a little ingenuity and imagination can often devise inexpensive visual aids that may prove more effective than expensive ones. What aids would you use to teach the facts about the moon? The earth, the moon, and the sun are difficult to visualize in the universe. How would you set up aids in your classroom as a representation of the earth, moon, and sun?

PART 1

SENSORY EXPERIENCE LEARNING: IN LIGHT OF RECENT RESEARCH

Introduction

Much recent research provides clarification regarding the mechanisms that form the basis for the sensory-learning process and that permits us to make a link between incoming sensory data and perception. The new information further informs us regarding how to approach sensory experience learning, and it fundamentally supports Carline's recommendations.

Some Definitions

Researchers in the field generally agree to a common definition of perception and perceptual learning. In general, it is said that perception refers to the process of taking in, organizing, and interpreting sensory information. Bahrick, Lickliter, and Flom (2004) noted "the fact that senses provide overlapping, redundant information from objects and events in the environment is therefore no extravagance of nature. Moreover, from our perspective, it is a cornerstone of perceptual development" (99).

Gibson (1969) focused on sensory or perceptual learning and the neural mechanisms that underpin the process and shared the following:

> Perceptual learning refers to an increase in the ability to extract information from the environment, as a result of experience and practice with stimulation coming from it. That the change should be in the direction of getting better information is a reasonable expectation, since man has evolved in the world and constantly interacts with it. Adaptive modification of perception should result in better correlation with events and objects that are sources of stimulation as well as an increase in the capacity to utilize potential stimulation. (3–4)

Perceptual learning then refers to learning improved perceptual skills. The process can involve the five sensory modalities and can include simple discriminations, as well as more complex activities. Perceptual learning forms important foundations of complex cognitive processes, such as language, and interacts with other kinds of learning that result in greater perceptual expertise (Kellman 2002, 259). According to Karni and Sagi (1991), the ability for perceptual learning is retained throughout life.

McGraw, Webb, and Moore (2009) discussed sensory learning and the neural mechanisms that support this process. Given the great interest and number of studies in this area, their goal was to examine and connect the various investigations that collectively increase understanding of this topic. They shared:

> Different levels of investigation have the potential to inform each other and create situations where step changes in understanding can be made. Detailed knowledge of how sensory learning changes the neurochemistry of the brain is likely to suggest novel pharmacological and behavioural interventions for various neurological deficits. Conversely, the success of therapeutic interventions, or lack of it, will provide crucial information on the nature and characteristics of the neural mechanisms underlying the learning process. (279)

Further, they shared that learning about objects often involves more than a single sense, apparent when a child examines an object for the first time. As McGraw et al. (2009) indicated, "Repeated viewing of the object from different angles is combined with coordinated tactile exploration using the hands (and often the mouth)" (281).

Sensory Processing

Sensory processing generally refers to taking in and interpreting information received from the environment. According to Thompson and Raisor (2013), "Sensory processing refers to taking in information through the senses" (34). Further, they indicated that while engaging in activities, children differ in their ability to process and respond to information from the environment. Teachers, therefore, need to understand sensory processing in order to meet each child's unique needs.

Patterns of Sensory Processing

As described in Dunn's model (Dunn 1997), sensory processing can be presented and discussed in a model with four patterns. The two dimensions of neurological threshold and behavioral response combine to form the four patterns of sensory processing in the model. Dunn (1997) indicated that patterns of sensory processing are used to determine a child's processing profile to describe how sensory processing occurs through the intersection of two dimensions. In addition, Dunn (2007) hypothesized that sensory processing occurs through that intersection of the two dimensions: the child's neurological threshold and the child's behavioral response to the environment. With knowledge of the patterns of sensory processing, teachers can structure classrooms to meet children's sensory needs. Teachers should address each child's pattern of sensory processing to help the child adapt to the classroom environment. Then, through observing the children's behaviors in response to that environment, a teacher can determine each child's processing profile and design better activities and interventions to support the child (Dunn 1997).

According to Dunn (2007), neurological thresholds that refer to the way the nervous system responds to sensory input and self-regulation strategies that refer to how individuals manage the input available to them or the regulation strategies that they use help us understand sensory processing. With regard to the relationship between neurological thresholds and self-regulation strategies, Dunn (1997) identified four basic patterns of sensory processing: (1) sensation seeking, a combination of high neurological threshold and an active self-regulation strategy. With sensation-seeking patterns of sensory processing, individuals enjoy active hands-on tasks and visual stimulation. Further, they seek and/or create sensory experiences for themselves; (2) sensation avoiding or a combination of low neurological threshold and an active self-regulation strategy or response. Individuals with a sensation-avoiding pattern withdraw from those situations with input that may bother them; (3) sensory sensitivity or a combination of low neurological threshold and a passive self-regulation strategy or response. Individuals with a sensory-sensitivity pattern tend to be reactive in situations and detect more input than others. Children with this pattern are generally distractible or more easily distracted and notice more sensory events than others; and (4) low registration or a combination of high neurological threshold and a passive self-regulation strategy. Individuals with low registration notice sensory stimuli much less than others and miss things in their environments.

Given this perspective, we can better understand how a person responds to sensory input and the self-regulation strategies that he or she uses. With increased understanding and accurate interpretation, those who design and implement educational strategies can create a better learning environment; that is, one that is more conducive to student learning.

Classroom Structure

In light of the patterns of sensory processing and responsiveness, it is important to structure the classroom to meet children's sensory needs. Since how each child responds to sensory information is related to sensory integration (Lynch and Simpson 2004), it is important to understand sensory integration when structuring the learning environment. Lynch and Simpson (2004) referred to sensory integration as ability to use sensory information from sound, lights, motion, and gravity and from tactile information in order to respond appropriately to the environment. Some sensory integration can be addressed by helping children develop self-regulation. Self-regulation refers to one's capacity to control one's impulses. As defined by Bodrova and Leong (2007), self-regulation involves controlling one's impulses and delaying gratification, which provides a basis for learning. Certain strategies can facilitate the development of children's self-regulation, such as helping children create and follow guidelines for the classroom and posting reminders of those guidelines in various creative ways (Bodrova and Leong 2005).

In order to structure the classroom to meet the needs of each child, since the way a child responds to sensory information is related to the level of integration, and in light of the fact that each child may respond differently, educators should focus on creating a multisensory environment. Many educators do understand that multisensory environments can help develop the five senses, improve motor development, and increase learning, and it is widely held that such environments promote development of language and social skills. In addition, Pitts (2012) indicated that using multiple senses allows more cognitive connections and associations to be made with a concept. Doing so helps children remember and retain information more effectively. Teachers, therefore, need to include activities that stimulate multiple senses.

Classroom Application

As Carline suggested, learning situations require development of visual percepts and percepts of sound, growth and motion, position, kinesthesia, and even taste and smell, when appropriate. While in the classroom, teachers need to build students' backgrounds through sensory experience learning and provide a multisensory environment in order to ensure development of required percepts.

Classroom procedures must account for and nurture students' natural tendency for perceptual learning (Kellman 2002). Demonstrating an example of classroom application, Kellman and colleagues showed that perceptual learning can be systematically produced and accelerated using specific computer-based technology. He and his colleagues used an approach to perceptual learning methods that involved mapping algebraic transformations. The experiment was set up to assess the effects of perceptual learning techniques on learners' speed and accuracy in recognizing algebraic transformations and the transfer of perceptual learning improvement to improvement in information extraction to algebra problem solving. It was demonstrated that when students practiced classifying algebraic transformations using the perceptual learning modules, they demonstrated significant improvement in terms of accuracy and response time in algebra problem solving. Kellman (2002) noted that perceptual learning training/practice can accelerate improvement on various dimensions of learning in the classroom.

Visual and Auditory Perception

When creating a classroom with a multisensory environment that is conducive to learning and when arranging for appropriate learning activities, it is important to focus on visual and auditory perception and related subskills, as they are closely linked with learning to read, write, and complete mathematical operations. These basic skills are essential for continued conceptual learning, problem solving, and critical thinking. As a reading specialist, I can say with certainty that reading skills serve as a foundation for much later learning.

Visual perception processing refers, in general, to one's ability to interpret what one sees. A component of visual perception processing is referred to as visual spatial skills. Linn and Peterson (1985) defined spatial ability as skill in "representing, transforming, generating, and recalling symbolic, nonlinguistic information" (1482). They described three categories of spatial ability: (1) spaced perception or ability to determine spatial relationships with regard to the orientation of one's own body; (2) mental rotation (rapidly and accurately rotate a two- or three-dimensional figure); and (3) spatial visualization that involves complicated multistep manipulation of spatially presented information (1482–1484).

Another aspect of visual perception processing consists of visual analysis/discrimination skills that enable one to identify, organize, and recall information presented visually. Visual analysis skills enable one to recognize features related to a visual stimulus (Sincero 2013b). A person with visual discrimination problems may reverse letters or numbers when writing them or may confuse certain letters, such as *b* and *d* or *p* and *q*, when reading. Sincero (2013b) described visual analysis/discrimination subskills as (1) figure ground, or attending to a form while disregarding other information; (2) visual form recognition/discrimination and constancy, or identifying the differences in features and form and recognizing that a form or shape is the same, even when its properties, such as size, have changed; (3) visual closure, or determining the appearance of a final form with missing details; (4) visual spatial memory or recall of the spatial location of an object/stimulus; (5) visual sequential memory, or recall of a sequence of numbers, letters or objects in the order they were previously presented; (6) visualization, or ability to create a mental image of an object seen earlier and mentally manipulate it; and (7) visual speed and span, or the amount and rate handled in visual processing. Feagans and Merriwether (1990) studied children with learning disabilities who demonstrated visual discrimination problems when they were six or seven years of age. They found that these children were less proficient in reading and in academic achievement, in general, when compared with other children with learning disabilities and when compared with normally achieving children, thus stressing the importance of visual discrimination for reading.

Woodrome and Johnson (2009) closely investigated visual perceptual skills that appear to be essential to letter learning. In particular, they studied the relevance of visual discrimination to the learning-to-read process. They found a specific relationship between visual discrimination and letter identification abilities, essential in the early stages of learning to read. Results of a pilot study that was conducted suggested that letter-name training did have an impact on letter identification of lower-case letters, but visual discrimination training did not positively affect performance. Woodrome and Johnson (2009) recommended that future research be conducted to demonstrate the hypothesized mediating effects of later knowledge on the relationship between visual discrimination and knowledge of letter-sound correspondence.

Foulin (2005) noted that it has been widely established that a major longitudinal predictor of learning to read in an alphabetic writing system is the knowledge of letter names. Given that letters serve fundamental functions in alphabetic writing systems, any aspect of letter knowledge might be expected to contribute to the acquisition of alphabetic literacy. Foulin (2005) indicated that many have recognized letter-sound knowledge as a requirement for acquiring the alphabetic principle that refers to the notion that letters in print essentially stand for phonemes in speech.

Treiman, Sotak, and Bowman (2001) addressed the roles of letter names and letter sounds in connecting print and speech. Marinelli and colleagues (2012), when focusing on the variables that affect the acquisition of reading skills, indicated that letter knowledge is critical in early reading and spelling because it shapes the acquisition of the alphabetic principle and of grapheme-to-phoneme correspondences. Treiman et al. (2001) also found that even adults take advantage of letter names when learning to read new words.

A third aspect of visual perception processing consists of visual integration skills that involve taking in, remembering, and applying the skills. According to Sincero (2013a), visual integration enables a person to combine one piece of sensory information with another of the same sense or a group of sensory information items of one sense with information of another sense. Sincero (2013a) described several aspects of visual integration: (1) visual-visual integration skill that involves joining several visual skills, enabling one, for example, to match a new word with an appropriate mental image; (2) visual-motor integration that enables one to incorporate visual information and motor sensory information; and (3) visual-auditory integration that enables one to coordinate visual information and sound information. Included are memory, discrimination, attention, closure, and figure-ground skills.

Also important in the learning-to-read process is auditory perception, generally understood as the ability to identify, interpret, and link meaning to sound. When one hears a sound, one interprets it to make sense of it. Sutaria (1985) noted several components of auditory perception. Auditory discrimination, or the ability to hear similarities and differences between sounds, enables one, for example, to distinguish between the words "pen" and "pin" and between "big" and "pig." Auditory foreground and background differentiation, or the ability to select and focus on relevant auditory stimuli, enables one, for example, to hear a teacher's voice, even when students' voices can be heard in the general area. Auditory blending, or auditory analysis and synthesis, the ability to synthesize individual sounds that form a word, enables one, for example, to break apart an unknown word into syllables and blend them to say a whole word such as "sat-is-fy." Auditory sequencing, or ability to remember the order of individual sounds in a specific stimulus, enables one, for example, to carry out directions that were provided orally, in the order they were presented. In addition, Sutaria (1985) indicated that children with auditory perception problems may appear to ignore verbal directions and ask that they be repeated, demonstrate poor speech patterns, and/or prefer visual tasks.

Mueller, Friederici, and Mannel (2012) noted that basic auditory perception may be an "important determinant of language learning processes across the range of normal and abnormal development" (15953). They indicated, "There is empirical evidence supporting the idea that early auditory abilities impact on later outcomes of language development in normal infants and populations with language-related disorders" (Mueller et al. 2012, 15953). In their study, they demonstrated "that basic auditory discrimination skills are linked to the learning of a simple grammatical rule in a population of healthy infants and adults" (Mueller et al., 15953). They used pitch perception as a test for auditory perceptual function. The findings of their study "show a clear relation between an electrophysiological measure of pitch discrimination and the ability of infants, and also adults, to extract a linguistic rule" (Mueller et al. 2012, 15955).

Rosner and Simon (1971, August/September) reported on the Auditory Analysis Test (AAT) that was developed to test auditory perception. This test was given to 284 children in K–6 classrooms. Correlations of individual AAT scores with Stanford Achievement Test reading scores yielded significant relationships. This test led to ways to address auditory perceptual dysfunction.

Auditory Processing

Visual and auditory perception abilities are essential to the learning-to-read process, and auditory processing is a key factor in this process. According to Stredler-Brown and Johnson (2004), auditory processing generally refers to the process of taking in sound through the ear and interpreting the information heard. Some skills are considered essential for auditory processing, including skills such as auditory discrimination, short-term auditory memory, and linguistic auditory processing (Stredler-Brown and Johnson 2004). Auditory processing includes phonological awareness.

Phonological Processing and Phonological and Phonemic Awareness

Phonological processing and phonological and phonemic awareness also play a central role in the learning-to-read process. Wagner and Torgesen (1987) indicated, "Phonological processing refers to the use of phonological information (i.e., the sounds of one's language) in processing written and oral language" (192). It involves ability to perceive and understand the speech sounds that make up syllables and words. According to Molfese, Molfese, and Molfese (2007), research demonstrates that both language and reading abilities have their origin in phonological skills that occur at various levels including awareness, retrieval, and memory. Due to several factors, children develop perceptual abilities that respond to speech and its variations. They noted that while most people demonstrate certain perceptual abilities that enable them to discriminate speech sounds in similar ways, others with weak perceptual skills do not process sound elements in usual or typical ways. The basic differences in perceptual skills may provide the basis for detecting potential language and reading problems (Molfese et al. 2007).

Building from these speech and perception skills are the phonological skills that are essential to the core ability for developing reading skills (Fletcher et al. 1999). According to Snowling and Hulme (1994), development of phonological skills "refers to the processes used by children to acquire and use the sound patterns of their native language in communication" (21). Application of phonological skills in reading includes decoding words or applying knowledge of letter-sound relationships to correctly pronounce words.

Lonigan (2006) noted, "There is now considerable evidence that phonological processing skills play a key role in acquiring reading and spelling in alphabetic languages" (77). He shared that research on phonological processing, which requires manipulation of the sounds in words, using various populations and diverse methods, has led to findings that link normal acquisition of reading skill and phonological awareness. Further, Lonigan (2006) indicated, "Taken together, these findings, similar to those for older children, indicate that phonological processing skills—at least phonological awareness—and letter knowledge are important determinants of early reading acquisition for children when measured in preschool and kindergarten" (81). In addition, Lonigan (2006) noted that evidence suggests "a reciprocal relationship between phonological processing skills and letter knowledge in preschoolers. Having more letter knowledge promotes the development of higher levels of phonological awareness, and having higher levels of phonological awareness, or phonological processing skills generally, promotes the development of letter knowledge" (84).

An aspect of phonological processing is phonological awareness. According to Mattingly (1972), phonological awareness basically refers to one's awareness of and access to the phonology of one's language. In general, phonological awareness refers to the ability to hear sounds of the words in spoken language and to recognize that words consist of various units of sound. As children develop phonological awareness, they understand that words consist of small units of sound (phonemes) and that words can be broken into syllables or larger segments of sound (Brummitt-Yale 2008). According to Melby-Lervag, Lyster, and Hulme (2012), "Phonological awareness refers to an individual's ability to reflect upon and manipulate the sound structure of spoken words" (323). Wagner and Torgesen (1987) indicated that for those with well-developed phonological awareness, "our alphabetic system, which conveys language at the phonological level, is a reasonable approach to visually representing our spoken language" (192).

Brunswick, Martin, and Rippon (2012) examined how phonological awareness, phonological memory, and visuospatial ability contribute to reading development in 142 English-speaking children from the start of kindergarten to the middle of second grade. They found that these skills are necessary for developing reading skills, but they did note that their relative importance varies across the first two years of reading development.

Phonics, which relies on phonological awareness, refers to making the connection between sounds and print. Understanding and making this connection are essential to the process of learning how to read.

Another aspect of phonological processing is phonemic awareness that involves the phoneme or smallest unit of sound. Brummitt-Yale (2008) indicated that readers with strong phonemic awareness demonstrate the ability to hear rhyme and alliteration (repetition of the same consonant sound at the beginning of different words used in various contexts) and to identify the different sound in a set of words, such as "bat" and "bad," and blend and segment phonemes. Phonemic awareness has a central or pivotal role as a predictor of individual differences in reading development (Melby-Lervag et al. 2012).

In addition, aspects of written language abilities have been highly correlated with reading skills overall. Hammill (2004) analyzed results of three meta-analyses that examined the extent to which a variety of measures of specific abilities are related to reading performance and, in the process, reviewed over 450 studies and analyzed nearly eleven thousand different coefficients. It was concluded that the most accurate and dependable predictors of reading ability are written language abilities, or abilities that involve print, such as word recognition and comprehension. Abilities that correlate with strong reading skills overall include those associated with the English writing system and abilities to associate speech sounds with letters, sound out and pronounce words, comprehend print, and read with accuracy and speed. Hammill (2004) noted that strong readers also tend to perform well on other print tasks, including spelling, punctuation, composing sentences, and writing compositions.

Implications for the Classroom

Much research focuses on classroom applications when addressing the improvement of reading skills. According to a report prepared by Diamond and Mandel (1996), research has demonstrated the importance of a systematic and research-based instructional approach with two essential elements:

"teaching the system of language and linking instruction in a logical sequenced progression throughout the grades" (4). They noted in this report that such an approach is part of a broader language-rich program that reflects the best practices of whole language. As a consequence, they encouraged teacher education programs to focus on how the English language system works, how children learn to read, and on the best practices for both skill development and whole-language activities. This report specifically suggested that all successful early reading programs "base instruction on accurate diagnostic information; develop print concepts; develop knowledge of letter names and shapes; convey that spoken words are composed of sounds (phonemic awareness); provide systematic and explicit instruction in sound/symbol relationships (phonics); connect that instruction to practice in highly decodable text that includes the sounds and symbols taught; make use of rich and varied literature and read to children regularly" (5). Diamond and Mandel (1996) noted that research findings indicate that phonemic awareness is the most formidable predictor of success in the learning-to-read process (6).

Sensory Experience Learning and a Multisensory Learning Environment

As Carline shared, teachers need to analyze how best to build background through sensory learning experiences and how to effectively foster recall of helpful percepts when designing new, complex learning experiences for their students. They need to understand the part that percepts play in learning, and if they find that the students' experiential backgrounds are insufficient, they must make provisions to build background. To do so, they should carefully design multisensory environments conducive to learning and based on student needs.

Today's research emphasizes the importance of designing instructional environments based on student needs, including each child's pattern of sensory processing, and on an understanding of sensory integration. In addition, the environments should reflect the research addressing perceptual learning and perception, patterns of sensory processing, and visual and auditory perception and processing, including phonological and phonemic awareness and phonological processing. Further, much research emphasizes the importance of implementing language-rich programs, including the use of various kinds of literature.

References for Part 1—Sensory Experience Learning

Bahrick, L. E., R. Lickliter, and R. Flom. 2004. "Intersensory Redundancy Guides the Development of Selective Attention, Perception, and Cognition in Infancy." *Current Directions in Psychological Science* 13, no. 3: 99–102.

Bodrova, E., and D. Leong. 2005. "Self-Regulation: A Foundation for Early Learning." *Principal* 85, no. 1: 30–35.

Bodrova, E., and D. J. Leong. 2007. *Tools of the Mind: The Vygotskian Approach to Early Childhood Education*. Upper Saddle River, NJ: Pearson.

Brummitt-Yale, J. 2008. "Phonemic Awareness vs. Phonological Awareness." *K–12 Reader: Reading Instruction Resources, 2008–2014*. www.k12reader.com/phonemic-awareness-vs-phonological-awareness.

Brunswick, N., G. N. Martin, and G. Rippon. 2012. "Early Cognitive Profiles of Emergent Readers: A Longitudinal Study." *Journal of Experimental Child Psychology* 111, no. 2: 268–285.

Diamond, L., and S. Mandel. 1996. *Building a Powerful Reading Program from Research to Practice*. Sacramento, CA: California State University Institute for Educational Reform. www.csus.edu/ier/reading.html.

Dunn, W. 1997. "The Impact of Sensory Processing Abilities on the Daily Lives of Young Children and Their Families: A Conceptual Model." *Infants and Young Children* 9, no.4: 23-35.

Dunn, W. 2007. "Supporting Children to Participate Successfully in Everyday Life by Using Sensory Processing Knowledge." *Infants and Young Children* 20, no. 2: 84–101.

Feagans, L.V., and A. Merriwether. 1990. "Visual Discrimination of Letter-Like Forms and Its Relationship to Achievement Over Time in Children with Learning Disabilities." *Journal of Learning Disabilities* 23, no. 7: 417–425. doi: 10.1177/002221949002300705.

Fletcher, J. M., B. R. Foorman, S. E. Shaywitz, and B. A. Shaywitz. 1999. "Conceptual and Methodological Issues in Dyslexia Research: A Lesson for Developmental Disorders." In *Neurodevelopmental Disorders*, edited by H. Tager-Flusberg, 271–306. Cambridge, MA: MIT Press.

Foulin, J. N. 2005. "Why Is Letter-Name Knowledge Such a Good Predictor of Learning to Read?" *Reading and Writing* 18, no. 2: 129–155. doi: 10.1007/s11145-004-5892-2.

Gates, A. I., A. T. Jersild, T. R. McConnell, and R. C. Challman. 1942. *Educational Psychology.* New York, NY: Macmillan Company.

Gibson, E. J. 1969. *Principles of Perceptual Learning and Development.* New York, NY: Appleton Century-Crofts.

Hammill, D. D. 2004. "What We Know about Correlates of Reading." *Exceptional Children* 70, no. 4: 453–468.

Karni, A., and D. Sagi. 1991. "Where Practice Makes Perfect in Texture Discrimination: Evidence for Primarily Visual Cortex Plasticity." *Proceedings of the National Academy of Sciences of the United States of America* 88, no. 11 (June): 4966–4970. doi: 10.1073/pnas.88.11.4966.

Kellman, P. J. 2002. "Perceptual Learning." In *Stevens' Handbook of Experimental Psychology: Learning, Motivation, and Emotion, Volume 3*, edited by H. Pashier and R. Gallistel, 259–299. New York, NY: John Wiley & Sons.

Linn, M. C., and A. C. Peterson. 1985. "Emergence and Characteristics of Sex Differences in Spatial Ability: A Meta-Analysis." *Child Development* 56, no. 6: 1479–1498.

Lonigan, C. J. 2006. "Conceptualizing Phonological Processing Skills in Prereaders." In *Handbook of Early Literacy Research, Volume 2*, edited by

D. K. Dickinson and S. B. Neuman, 77–89. New York, NY: Guilford Press.

Lynch, S., and C. Simpson. 2004. "Sensory Processing: Meeting Individual Needs Using the Seven Senses." *Young Exceptional Children* 7, no. 4: 2–9.

Marinelli, C. V., M. Martelli, P. Praphamontripong, P. Zoccolotti, and H. Abadzi. 2012. "Visual and Linguistic Factors in Literacy Acquisition: Instructional Implications for Beginning Readers in Low-Income Countries." *Global Partnership for Education Working Paper Series on Learning*, no. 2 (November): 1–166. Washington, DC: World Bank.

Mattingly, I. G. 1972. "Reading, the Linguistic Process, and Linguistic Awareness." In *Language by Ear and by Eye: The Relationship between Speech and Reading*, edited by J. F. Kavanagh and I. G. Mattingly, 133–147. Cambridge, MA: MIT Press.

McGraw, P.V., B.S. Webb, and D. R. Moore, 2009. "Introduction. Sensory Learning: From Neural Mechanisms to Rehabilitation." *Philosophical Transactions of the Royal Society of London B: Biological Sciences* 364 (February): 279–283. doi: 10.1098/rstb.2008.0274.

Melby-Lervag, M., S. A. Lyster, and C. Hulme. 2012. "Phonological Skills and Their Role in Learning to Read: A Meta-Analytic Review." *Psychological Bulletin* 138, no. 2: 322–352.

Molfese, D., V. Molfese, and P. Molfese. 2007. "Relation between Early Measures of Brain Responses to Language Stimuli and Childhood Performance on Language and Language-Related Tasks." In *Human Behavior, Learning, and the Developing Brain: Atypical Development*, edited by D. Coch, G. Dawson, and K. W. Fisher, 191–211. New York, NY: Guilford Publications, Inc.

Mueller, J. L., A. D. Friederici, and C. Mannel. 2012. "Auditory Perception at the Root of Language Learning." In *Proceedings of the National Academy of Sciences of the United States of America* 109, no. 39 (September), edited by M. Merzenich and W. M. Keck, 15953–15958. San Francisco, CA: Center for Integrative Neuroscience. doi: 10.1073/pnas.1204319109.

Pitts, A. 2012. "Learning is Multisensory: How to Engage All the Senses so Children Really Benefit." (December). HowToLearn.com.

Rosner, J., and D. P. Simon. 1971. "The Auditory Analysis Test: An Initial Report." *Journal of Learning Disabilities* 4, no. 7: 384–392. doi: 10.1177/002221947100400706.

Sincero, S. A. 2013a. "Visual Integration Skills." http://explorable.com/visual-integration-skills.

Sincero, S. A. 2013b. "Visual Analysis Skills." http://explorable.com/visual-analysis-skills.

Snowling, M., and C. Hulme. 1994. "The Development of Phonological Skills." *Philosophical Transactions of the Royal Society B: Biological Sciences* 346, no. 1315: 21–27.

Stredler-Brown, A., and C. D. Johnson. 2004. *Functional Auditory Performance Indicators: An Integrated Approach to Auditory Skill Development.* www.cde.state.co.us/cdesped/download/pdf/FAPI 3-1-04g.pdf.

Sutaria, S. D. 1985. *Specific Learning Disabilities: Nature and Needs.* Springfield, IL: Charles C. Thomas.

Thompson, S. D., and J. M. Raisor. 2013. "Meeting the Sensory Needs of Young Children." *Young Children* (May): 34–43.

Treiman, R., L. Sotak, and M. Bowman. 2001. "The Roles of Letter Names and Letter Sounds in Connecting Print and Speech." *Memory and Cognition* 29, no. 6: 860–873.

Wagner, R. K., and J. K. Torgesen. 1987. "The Nature of Phonological Processing and Its Causal Role in the Acquisition of Reading Skills." *Psychological Bulletin* 101, no. 2: 192–212.

Woodrome, S. E., and K. E. Johnson. 2009. "The Role of Visual Discrimination in the Learning-to-Read Process." *Reading and Writing* 22 (February): 117–131.

PART 2

MEMORY-TYPE LEARNING: TIMELESS WISDOM

Introduction

Perhaps the most frequently used type of learning in our schools is the memory type of learning. With regard to this type of learning, it is important to investigate the products of learning called prompt mental responses. These responses are so thoroughly fixed in mind that they can be used promptly when situations that require them arise. One's name, the days of the week, the months of the year, famous dates in history, correct spelling, poems, rules in mathematics, names of persons and things, and facts of various kinds are examples of prompt mental responses. Those who provide prompt mental responses include the good speller who can spell a large number of words quickly and accurately; the student who is proficient with addition and multiplication and finds the right answers to such problems without delay; and a master teacher who recites poetry and quotations freely. Those who use information to meet such mental demands promptly and accurately have memorized it.

Knowing that there are and should be quick mental responses is the starting point in addressing this type of learning, but the major task is to examine the activities that should occur before prompt mental responses emerge as genuine end products.

Background Needed for Memorization

The names of states and their capitals, a rule in spelling, the positions in the president's cabinet, the rules for multiplying and dividing fractions, and words in songs to be sung in special programs are commonly memorized. I recall the comment of a fifth-grade student in a class that was asked to memorize "Stopping by the Woods on a Snowy Evening" by Robert Frost: "Well, if it must be memorized, the only thing left is for the teacher to tell us when it has to be learned, and then check up on us to see if we did it."

I sincerely hope that you will not hold the same viewpoint involving memorization (or prompt reproductions). Too many teaching obligations lie dormant under the unprofessional practice of assigning, checking up, and grading, rather than preparing students for what they are to memorize. In the last stanza of this poem, it is especially evident that activities of an entirely different kind should have preceded memorization. Wouldn't the memorization process have been much more proficient and meaningful if the teacher had said, "Share the author's feelings as you sense the quiet stillness of the snowy evening, as Robert Frost stops by the woods to watch them fill up with snow." A simpler quietness pervades every word, even to the last line that seems to end in a whisper.

As the poem closes, one becomes aware of the poet's ability to find meaning and wisdom in common things. "But I have promises to keep, and miles to go before I sleep." Perhaps something about the poem's author would add background in support of the memorization process. Biographical data is always beneficial, but sharing something revealing about the personality, philosophy, and intentions of the author is a powerful way to develop background for memorization. For example, the teacher could have told those children that Robert Frost had a passionate belief in poetry as a "way of expressing thoughts of the heart." And the teacher could have shared that the author also believed that "a poem begins in light and ends in wisdom." Robert Frost won the Pulitzer Prize four times. Young and old alike take delight in his poems of wit, wisdom, and tenderness. With such information, the children's memorization process would have been strongly supported.

Now let us assume that the positions in the president's cabinet are so vital that they should be memorized. The following describes how a sixth-grade social studies teacher led the class in the process. She said, "These positions you must know, so come prepared to recite them." She then gave the class a list of positions that everyone needed to recall. She proceeded by saying, "Each cabinet member is in charge of some important work that the government does for us or helps us to do. Between now and tomorrow, I want you to look around and see what important work you see people engaged in, right *here* in our town. Probably you will see some persons who work for the government, or you might see something relevant on television regarding international relations. Look on bottles of medicine and packages of food; examine the newspapers; watch for signs of US, as this sign means that the government is interested or involved."

The next day, the class, with the aid of the teacher, shared the following:

Pupils' Observations and Positions Named:

- Saw a one-dollar bill marked United States of America: **Secretary of the Treasury**
- President, in a message to Congress, discussed plans for strengthening the Department of Labor and suggested procedures for pursuing labor negotiations: **Secretary of Labor**
- Attorney General directed the United States Commission of Immigration and Naturalization to rewrite guidelines for acceptance of refugees from other countries: **Attorney General**
- Saw label with the words "Registered in the United States Patent Office"; Secretary of Commerce wrote a pamphlet called "The Common Market": **Secretary of Commerce**
- A cutback in military spending is imminent, according to a newspaper article: **Secretary of Defense**
- Read article about the Navy Department closing fifteen major naval bases in the Atlantic and the Pacific: **Secretary of the Navy**
- Saw a right-to-read article: **Secretary of Health, Education, and Welfare**
- Read article in the newspaper about the new secretary of state who traveled a million miles since entering government service: **Secretary of State**
- Bureau of Indian Affairs: **Secretary of Interior**
- Saw a truck marked US Mail and a building marked US Post Office with a sign announcing that stamps will increase two cents: **Postmaster General**
- Saw a photo of soldiers following a tank: **Secretary of the Army**
- Read an article about the soil bank land gradually disappearing: **Secretary of Agriculture**
- Saw a picture of a jet pilot in military uniform: **Secretary of the Air Force**

Using the findings of these children and expanding on their ideas, the teacher helped the pupils gain familiarity with the names of the cabinet positions and a few duties connected with each one. Further, pupils began to experience the proximity of the cabinet members' work to their own lives.

When the teacher tested for recall (memory) of these positions, the pupils responded remarkably well, largely because their memory work had been preceded with learning activities that fostered and supported recall. If possible, before asking youngsters to memorize, build up a background of meaning in which the material to be memorized can take root, grow, and hold fast.

Maximum Use of Background Possibilities

A background of meaning, of course, cannot be developed to the same degree with all materials and topics. Some materials have strong associations and meanings, but others have feeble background-producing possibilities. The tragic part, however, is that background may not be developed for memorization of material that *does* have deep and abundant associations and meanings. In teaching reading, for example, many teachers seem to think that the recitation of word symbols is the real test of accomplishment, whereas this reiteration may be only an echo of sounds from hollow places. Reiteration is too often only veneer. The shabby cloak of rote memory must not be worn and assumed to be a real garment; real learning cannot be imitated. Memorizing should be the fixation of facts and ideas after they are well understood.

Responses with Strong Background Possibilities

Many situations in school and in life require one to know and understand ideas, points, provisions, reasons, causes, or events and to recall them and their details quite promptly, although not as promptly as names, dates, rules, definitions, or other materials learned verbatim. Prompt mental responses that reflect rich and strong associations and meanings are required.

When building a background for these ideas and concepts in order to facilitate prompt responses, one should make a couple of considerations. First, it is important to understand the nature of the content that has strong background building possibilities. The content to be reduced to relatively prompt mental responses provides the answers to questions such as the following: What are the ways in which water is continuously reproduced? What are two reasons why one could make errors in addition? Enumerate the chief events in Smokie's life from the time he was a little range colt to the time Clint took him back to the range, where Smokie's heart again came to life. What reasons can you give for having a Congress with two houses—a House of Representatives and a Senate—rather than one? The responses to these kinds of questions will be different from responses to questions about dates, rules, definitions, or other data learned verbatim. Instead, because of implied associations, potential for summarization, and opportunity for respondents to express answers in their own words, the responses may vary in how they are expressed.

The following principle should guide activities preceding the memorization of material with strong background possibilities: *Build a strong background for the material to be memorized so it can take root, grow, and hold fast.* Focus attention on the *take root* and *grow* parts, as memorizing will be much easier and permanent if the background provided prior to memorization is well developed. In fact, it is through the background-building process that concepts/ideas to be memorized germinate, develop, and take strong root before the holding-fast part needs to be addressed.

One also should carefully identify information/material to be memorized. When or where in life is it a matter of reputation, honor, salary, bread and butter, promotion, youthfulness, or enjoyment that one must be able to recall in chronological order memorized events? In no other place but the classroom would such stilted situations typically be met. When or where in life is one required to memorize and have at one's fingertips the lines from various authors, poets, mathematicians, or historians? At no time and in no place except the classroom do we usually find such requirements. Some situations in life, however, require prompt mental responses to questions about material with strong background possibilities. In those situations, one needs to ingrain appropriate responses. The ideas should be welded together and grounded in a background of understanding so they can be promptly recalled. Such recall is reliant on the background wherein the ideas are deeply and firmly established.

Responses with Weak Background Possibilities

Even for material with feeble background possibilities, teachers should provide a hint, a suggestion, a percept, or a clue of some kind to build background. The names of states and their capitals can be memorized more easily, for example, if one gains a percept of them through their arrangement on a map or by thinking of them in terms of general location by sections or areas on the map, only because the percepts in these cases are more valuable than their verbal or written names. In general physical science, *Fe* for iron and the simple hint that Fe comes from the Latin word *ferrum* helps in forming a background for memory. Pupils can recall definitions, meaningful statements, and rules, reduced to prompt mental responses by hard and laborious memorizing, if they have some background to facilitate their learning and retention.

Activities Following Development of a Background

Having dwelt thus far on building a background as an essential activity for memorizing material, it is now important to focus on some additional pedagogically sound activities that facilitate memorization.

- ❐ Recall. This is the first activity that needs to be addressed. Recall is different from repetition. Repetition involves repeating an activity in order to stamp in the particular item to be learned. On the other hand, recall involves bringing up that information in one's mind with no external assistance. Can you recall the name of your third-grade teacher? Who was the valedictorian in your high school graduating class? Who became the US president following the death of Lincoln? It may be years since you were called upon to answer such questions. The activity you employ in bringing the answers to mind is called recall. Recall, as used here, can be employed also when memorizing information; that is, during the process of learning the material. While studying, children are inclined to look immediately in the textbook, notebook, or any source for the information as soon as a prompt response does not come to mind. Recall, however, involves bringing the response to mind by finding it in the background information. Recall should function during the process of memorizing. It exerts a pull that helps fix the information firmly in mind, and it is exactly the same activity that is exercised when memorized material is needed in the future.

    In directing children to use recall, the teacher should address how it is different for the two kinds of prompt mental responses. The first group of responses that don't require strong background development and that need exact and rapid reproduction relies on recall in a strict sense because the information is not amenable to connections/rich associations or individual ways of expression.

Information for which strong background has been developed, however, can be recalled by reliving or reexamining the conditions and circumstances that gave rise to the original ideas. Responses involve finding the information in the background that was developed.

- ❐ True-to-Use Activity. This is another activity that should be used during the process of memorization. For example, when learning to read, a child makes much greater progress if the words in print include words from the child's speaking and listening vocabulary. In short, children need to see words that they have used and/or heard. Often children are required to memorize words and their meanings based on the order in which they appear in their texts or from a vocabulary list or a serial arrangement. The true-to-use activity would have children learn the words that they can define. For example, a fifth-grade teacher whom I observed always put a list of words to be spelled on the chalkboard, and at the end of the day, she erased the words and dictated them in the same order as they had appeared on the chalkboard. Many of the children had the entire list of words written down on their spelling pads before the teacher was halfway through the list, and then these pupils sat motionless during the remainder of the dictation time. Noticing this practice (after several weeks of unawareness), the teacher, without warning, dictated the words in a mixed order. That day the spelling was significantly less accurate. Some of the children didn't know the meaning of the words in the list but had simply memorized the spelling of the words in the order provided. Using a true-to-use activity, the teacher would have created a list of words that the children had used or heard and/or the meanings of which had been discussed.

- ❐ Organization. The last activity to be addressed with regard to memorization involves the principle of organization. Many learning theorists call attention to learning by the whole, in contrast to learning by the parts, signifying that there are two methods to use when memorizing or a combination of both. A classic illustration is the learning of poetry. If children proceed in memorizing the words while reviewing the poem as a whole, they use the whole-method approach. If they memorize one stanza and then move on to the next until each stanza has been memorized and finally put each stanza in its proper place, they use the parts method. There may be no strict rule regarding which method—by the whole, by the parts, or by a combination of the two methods—to honor when directing learning. The teacher must use clues from the nature of the materials.

Why is a person able to remember a joke, even in great detail, after hearing it once? Why are some children able to relate the plot and development of a book after reading it? Why can a child go to a movie and then tell the complete story at home a few hours later? Yes, paying attention, having a good memory, and wanting to retain are good answers, but there is a deeper reason. The content of these materials can be pieced together easily. The pieces have grouping and developing possibilities. In short, these materials can be organized. Why, therefore, should they not be learned as one continuous unit, as a whole? The nature of the material plays a big part in determining how to direct memorizing.

Poems and stories, as a general rule, have some plot, story, event, or group of ideas that speak to organization. "Little Boy Blue," "Casey at the Bat," *Pippi Longstocking*, *The Story of Dr. Doolittle*, *Charlotte's Web*, "What Do We Plant?" "Cat," and "The Pasture" are examples of books and poems with organization possibilities. Lincoln's Gettysburg Address also reveals the organization of ideas. The principle governing memorizing in such cases can be stated as follows: *Whenever materials clearly and logically follow an organizational pattern, group the content into one continuous and complete whole, and learn the whole piece as a unit with an organized structure.*

I remember well a sad and tense picture of a fourth-grade girl delivering a memorized oration to parents gathered in the auditorium for the annual Christmas program. About halfway through the memorized oration, the child halted, looked around, blushed, twisted, and hoped, but no words came to her mind. She had forgotten the rest of her lines. After several minutes of quiet in that auditorium, she sat down and looked at the floor for the remainder of the program. After the program was over and the youngster left the stage, she cried pitifully. This little girl had memorized words. There was no meaning behind the words, meaning that may have helped her recall what to say. There was no organization of ideas to rely upon.

Probably this child should have had a few rounded and developed ideas, and for these she should have learned the organizational pattern while she fulfilled her long speaking part that night. More emphasis in memorizing, both prompt and relatively prompt responses, should be placed on the ideas and their organization, in contrast to searching for information/material that was memorized with no background of meaning and organization. Memorizing to recall prompt or relatively prompt mental responses is an important and often-used method for learning. Teachers should give attention especially to the activities that will, as far as possible, build a strong background so that content to be reduced to prompt responses can take root, grow, and hold fast. Also, they should place emphasis on the principles that can guide memorizing after the background has been developed or established.

Application Exercises

- ☐ Which will weigh more: a quart of ice cream or a quart of milk? Is there any good reason why one should endeavor to memorize which one is the heavier or the lighter? Could one, on the basis of background or experience, determine the relative weight of the quarts?
- ☐ What particular benefit comes from memorizing the capitals of the states? What is the capital of Vermont? Texas? Colorado? Washington? Hawaii?
- ☐ In a certain supermarket where people often pay by writing checks instead of using credit cards, the clerks always call a customer by the person's last name the second time the customer passes through the checkout stand. Can it be that clerks have good memories? How do you feel if a person introduced to you half a dozen times still cannot call you by name? Is it important to memorize names in the two cases described?
- ☐ Is there much background-building possibility for learning the colors in the spectrum or the number of days in the different months? Do you know of mnemonic devices that are helpful when one tries to recall the colors or the number of days in each month? Would you employ a nonsense word as a device to recall positions, order, or specific procedures? Why?

PART 2

MEMORY-TYPE LEARNING: IN LIGHT OF RECENT RESEARCH

Introduction

Since the late 1960s and early '70s, researchers have conducted numerous studies that inform us about memory-type learning and that identify a number of instructional strategies that align with various memory-type learning goals. Students must commit knowledge and skills to memory. They need to organize, retain, and retrieve information and skills on a regular basis. Banikowski and Mehring (1999) noted that memory is focused on learning, remembering, and using knowledge and skills. They indicated that for educators, memory is the only evidence of what students have learned. Since students must recall what they have learned in order to demonstrate their learning, it is essential to review memory theory and examine some strategies designed to enhance learning and memory. It becomes apparent when reviewing the literature that Carline's thinking and timeless wisdom are well supported.

Multistore Models

A traditional model of memory is known as the multistore model, such as the model described by Atkinson and Shiffrin (1968), in which memory is composed of a series of stores. In this model, the structural features of the memory system have three components: sensory register, short-term store, and long-term store. They acknowledged a close relationship between the short- and long-term store and indicated, "The short-term memory store may be regarded as the subject's 'working memory.' Information entering the short-term store is assumed to decay and disappear completely, but the time required for the information to be lost is considerably longer than for the sensory register" (92). Further, they noted that information in the long-term store does not decay and become lost in the same manner. "All information is eventually lost from the sensory register and short-term store, whereas information in the long-term store is relatively permanent (although it may be modified or rendered temporarily irretrievable as the result of other incoming information" (93).

Atkinson and Shiffrin (1968) indicated that some information is transferred to the long-term store throughout an item's stay in the short-term store, but the amount and form of the information transferred relies on the control processes and coding strategy used. Essentially, they presented a theoretical framework for memory that emphasized the role of control processes or processes controlled by the individual, such as rehearsal, coding, and search strategies.

In discussing this model, McLeod (2007a) indicated that information detected by sense organs enters "sensory memory." Information that is attended to enters into the short-term memory and then transfers to the long-term memory but only if the information is rehearsed. The focus initially was on maintenance rehearsal, but later it was suggested that rehearsal could include elaborative rehearsal. Information that is not rehearsed is lost from short-term memory through displacement or decay.

It was later thought that multistore models were oversimplified. McLeod (2007a) noted, "The model is oversimplified, in particular when it suggests that both short-term and long-term memory each operate in a single, uniform manner" (10). Further, many in the field concluded that both short- and long-term memory may be far more complex than initially described.

Working Memory Model

Baddeley and Hitch (1974) developed an alternative model of short-term memory that they called "working memory." As Baddeley (2012) noted, "The term 'working memory' evolved from the earlier concept of short-term memory (STM), and the two are still on occasion used interchangeably" (4). He explained that in the Baddeley and Hitch model, working memory implies both storage and manipulation, whereas short-term memory in earlier multistore models referred to simple temporary storage of information. In their model, short-term memory includes different components rather than a single store. Baddeley (2012) noted that essentially, they "abandoned the assumption that working memory comprised a single unitary store, proposing instead a three-component system: central executive, visuo-spatial sketch pad and phonological loop" (6). In this model, the system is not unitary but is divided into an executive component with two temporary storage systems, one for speech and sound and another for visuo-spatial. In describing the working memory model, McLeod (2012) indicated that working memory is short-term memory, but information doesn't go into a single store, as there are different systems for different kinds of information.

While the initial model that Baddeley and Hitch described in 1974 included three components, Baddeley in 2000 added a fourth component called the "episodic buffer." Baddeley (2012) described this component as one that permits "the original model to take account of the evidence of links between working memory and long-term memory" (11). He explained that "it is episodic in that it is assumed to hold integrated episodes or chunks in multidimensional code. In doing so, it acts as a buffer store, not only between the components of working memory, but also linking working memory to perception and long-term memory" (15).

Although Baddeley and Hitch's working memory model may have replaced Atkinson and Shiffrin's short-term memory store, Baddeley (2012) noted that further research is being conducted on neurobiological approaches to working memory and some alternative approaches that are somewhat consistent with the working memory approach. According to McLeod (2012), the Baddeley and Hitch model focuses on short-term memory and does not clearly address the sensory register and long-term memory, so it isn't a comprehensive memory model.

Information Processing Models

Some other models that address memory are information processing models. McLeod (2008) indicated that information processing is viewed by cognitive psychologists as a model of how human thought works, and Huitt (2003) shared that a primary focus of cognitive psychology, a major approach in psychology today, is on memory. There seems to be general consensus among cognitive psychologists about a number of aspects of the information processing system, including limited capacity, type of control system for stimuli, interaction of new information with stored information, and genetic traits that "dictate" the method by which individuals gain information (Lutz and Huitt 2003).

One well-known model of information processing is the stage theory model that is based on Atkinson and Shiffrin's multistore model of memory discussed above. Huitt (2003) indicated that in this model, information is processed and stored in three stages: sensory memory, short-term or working memory, and long-term memory. As noted in "Part 1—Sensory Experience Learning," individuals come into contact with information through the sensory receptors as they hear, see, taste, smell, and touch. Information, however, is only briefly stored in sensory memory. Lutz and Huitt (2003) indicated that memory in sensory memory is temporarily limited, in that it disappears quickly if not transferred to short-term memory, but attention and automaticity facilitate sensory memory. Further, they indicated that new information must be brought into memory in a meaningful way, or it will not be stored as memory. Several models of pattern recognition address how new stimuli are recognized in sensory memory. Ormrod (1998) noted also that attention plays a key role in moving information from the sensory register to working (short-term) memory. Because the capacity of human attention is limited, only some information that a person initially receives moves into working or short-term memory (Banikowski and Mehring 1999).

With regard to the second stage of information processing, short-term or working memory, Lutz and Huitt (2003) indicated that "this stage is often viewed as a conscious memory because it is the part of memory that is actively being processed while new information is being taken in" (4). They discussed two ways that are used for processing information when it is in short-term memory: rote or maintenance rehearsal and more complex elaboration or elaborative rehearsal. The latter is required to transfer information to long-term memory. As they pointed out, rote or maintenance rehearsal, which involves repetition, is insufficient for producing a lasting effect, and they noted that if information is not further processed, it will be lost. Eggen and Kauchak (1996) indicated there are basically three choices for working memory: disregard the information; retain the information by rehearsing it; or transfer the information to long-term memory through encoding the information or getting it into long-term memory so it can be recalled.

Long-term memory is the third stage of information processing. Banikowski and Mehring (1999) defined long-term memory as having three characteristics: long duration, unlimited capacity, and a rich network of interconnections among the pieces of information stored in long-term memory. They indicated that "long-term memory seems to be capable of holding as much information as an individual needs to store there" (5). Lutz and Huitt (2003) noted there are several categories of long-term memory, and different types of information are stored in long-term memory. They indicated the following:

> Today cognitive psychologists believe that there are at least different types of information stored in long-term memory. Each of the memory structures is distinct and serves a different operational function. However, it is evident that some type of very specialized categorization system exists within the human mind. (5)

Lutz and Huitt (2003) described declarative memory as memory that can be verbalized and that can be subdivided into semantic and episodic memories. The semantic memory store includes facts, concepts, principles, and problem-solving skills and strategies. The episodic memory store includes personal experiences and specific events. Slavin (1997) indicated that episodic memory involves memory of what we have seen or heard, such as details of a prior event that we attended. In addition to declarative memory, Lutz and Huitt (2003) discussed procedural memory. The procedural memory store includes memories of how to do something, such as a physical task like driving or riding a bicycle that may have reached a state of automaticity when attention requirements are minimal, as little awareness or conscious effort is required.

In addition to the stage theory model, there are other information processing theories. One that has received much attention is the levels-of-processing model. Craik and Lockhart (1972), who also questioned the adequacy of multistore models of memory, developed a levels-of-processing model in contrast to the stage model. In terms of the levels-of-processing model, they questioned the concepts of capacity limitations, coding, and the retention function. They indicated:

> We prefer to think of memory tied to levels of perceptual processing. Although these levels may be grouped into stages (sensory analyses, pattern recognition, and stimulus elaboration, for example), processing levels may be more usefully envisaged as a continuum of analyses. Thus, memory, too, is viewed as a continuum from the transient products of sensory analyses to the highly durable products of semantic-associative operations. (676)

The levels of processing model that Craik and Lockhart developed focuses on the processes involved in memory, as opposed to short-term and long-term memory and the idea that the manner in which information is encoded affects how well it is remembered (Craik and Lockhart 1972). As McLeod (2007b) noted, they viewed memory as a "by-product" of the depth of processing of information with no clear distinction between short-term and long-term memory. Craik and Lockhart (1972) indicated that deeper processing leads to improved memory. In their view, the levels of processing framework includes "a series or 'hierarchy' of processing stages referred to as 'depth of processing' where greater depth implies a greater degree of semantic or cognitive analysis" (675). Deep processing, then, implies more meaningful analysis of information and leads to greater recall. They saw memory tied to levels of perceptual processing or as a processing system with memory viewed as a continuum, as opposed to the multistore approach that includes sensory stores, short-term memory, and long-term memory or separate stores of information.

Later research demonstrated that processing is more complex and varied than described in Craik and Lockhart's levels-of-processing model, but as McLeod (2007b) noted, their work with this model drove much further memory research that has informed us today.

As noted by Lutz and Huitt (2003), the levels-of-processing model was a precursor to the development of the schema theory of information processing and memory, sometimes referred to as the connectionist model or theory. Further, they noted another theory in information processing, the dual coding theory, that "gives equal significance to both verbal and non-verbal processing and suggests that there are two separate systems for processing these types of information" (8).

How Children's Brains Memorize Facts

Researchers have conducted significant work that focuses on the brain and the learning process, or how children perceive and process new information, and on how children's brains memorize facts. An example of recent research is a study that was designed to determine the hippocampal system's contribution to the transition from procedure-based to memory-based problem-solving strategies (Qin et al. 2014). This brain imaging research illustrates the functional maturation of brain systems that underlie the transition from use of counting to memory-based retrieval during arithmetic problem solving. According to the study, brain changes, many involving the hippocampus or memory center, are central to the transformation. The hippocampus provides a scaffold for learning and consolidates facts into long-term memory. Findings of the study point to the "dynamic role of the hippocampus in the maturation of memory-based problem solving and establishes a critical link between hippocampal-neocortical reorganization and children's cognitive development" (Qin et al. 2014, 1263). They noted that this study "provides new insights into the mechanisms through which hippocampal-neocortical functional reorganization promotes the shift from use of effortful procedure-based to more efficient memory-based problem solving from childhood through adolescence into adulthood" (Qin et al. 2014, 1269).

As Bonnema (2009) noted, research of this kind describes the biological and physiological aspects involved in learning, but it may be even more important for teachers to understand how students "functionally" learn and to gain information about how to teach so that students understand and remember information. The following section, therefore, focuses on strategies that teachers can implement in order to enhance learning and memory.

Enhancing Learning and Memory—Based on Brain-Based Research

In light of the models of memory, particularly the well-known information processing stage theory model, it is understood that information is processed in essentially three stages: sensory memory, short-term or working memory, and long-term memory, as described earlier (Huitt 2003). Certain strategies are available to teachers to facilitate learning and memory at each of these stages. As indicated in "Part 1—Sensory Experience Learning: In Light of Recent Research," teachers need to carefully design multisensory environments that are conducive to learning and that reflect research addressing perceptual learning and perception, patterns of sensory processing, and visual and auditory perception and processing, including phonological processing and awareness and phonemic awareness. Presenting information to multiple senses enables one to more effectively process information. As noted in the earlier discussion on information processing models, Ormrod (1998) and Banikowski and Mehring (1999) indicated that attention is a key factor in moving information from the sensory register to working (short-term) memory, but the limited capacity of human attention enables only some information received to move to short-term memory. According to Bonnema (2009), factors such as attention, meaning, and emotion help to shift sensory memory into a "lower gear," enabling the learner to better scrutinize incoming data. Memory in sensory memory either disappears or is transferred to short-term or working memory.

Further, attention plays a key role in enhancing retention in working memory, as well as in moving information from the sensory register to working memory. In order to extend processing time in working memory, it is important to increase students' attention. Stanny (2009) noted the importance of paying attention, as students remember what they process and attend to. Banikowski and Mehring (1999) stressed that the first step in learning and remembering critical information is to pay attention, so it is important to gain students' attention when presenting a topic. They suggested providing an emotional "hook"; strategies to connect students emotionally with a topic include using a game format, music or drama; using tangible instructional devices or visual aids, such as charts, maps or models; using pictures or illustrations to facilitate connection with a topic; and organizing debates, discussions, or role-playing scenarios. Also, they indicated that it's necessary to create a positive emotional climate to facilitate attention to learning. Providing emotional "hooks" is consistent with creating a positive emotional climate (Banikowski and Mehring 1999).

Bogue (1993) noted that classroom teachers often gain students' attention by signaling to them that important information is about to be provided. Given these cues, students know that they should pay attention to specific points about to be addressed. When delivering presentations or lectures, teachers should, and often do, provide signals in several ways:

- Introduce the topic by saying, "Today, we are going to discuss …"
- Use words introducing statements of importance, such as "An important feature …"; "The chief reason …"; "You should remember that …"; or "It's important to know that …"
- Use words signaling definitions of terms before giving actual definitions by saying something like "The definition is …"; "It is called …"; or "is referred to as …"
- Use words that introduce lists by telling students what the items in the lists are about by saying, "There are many reasons …"; "The five

steps are as follows"; or "There are a number of ways …." Each item in a list may be signaled by words such as "first, second, third" or "first, next, then, finally."
- ❐ Change speed and volume by slowing down and speaking louder or dropping their voices to stress a point.
- ❐ Use words at the end of presentations or lectures, such as "To summarize …" or "Let's review what we have covered today."
- ❐ Point out key terms when making presentations; when discussing other visual aids such as maps, charts and sketches; and when writing on the whiteboard.

Given such cues, students are alerted that important information is being provided or will follow and should be noted.

In the classroom, it is important also to build background or provide students with information about a topic before presenting new information, as Carline suggested. Teachers need to ensure that they build a strong background for students in order to enhance working memory. Sufficient knowledge better enables a person to organize new information in working memory and move it to long-term memory (Kuhara-Kojima and Hatano 1991). Even when working with relatively homogeneous groups of students, however, teachers need to understand that the capacity of working memory for carrying out learning tasks differs among students. Some of the difference is due to the different levels of background knowledge that enhance this capacity.

Further, there are some specific strategies that facilitate activating students' prior knowledge and experience with a topic. Having prior knowledge or experience that relates to current learning enhances memory (Banikowski and Mehring 1999). Teachers can uncover students' prior knowledge and link the new information to it, or they can provide knowledge/background needed when students have no prior knowledge or experience, as discussed earlier. Brainstorming strategies are excellent examples of what teachers can use to activate students' prior knowledge and experience with a topic, as brainstorming leads students to identify what they already know about a topic and what they have learned after the topic is presented.

In addition to brainstorming, other strategies for uncovering students' prior knowledge, particularly applicable when assigning written material, are prereading techniques (Langer 1981; Langer 1982; Bogue 1993). Such techniques ask students to convert headings in printed material into questions, contemplate and discuss what they already know about the topic and the questions raised, and read to find the answers and additional information.

While gaining students' attention, building background, and activating students' prior knowledge in order to enhance retention of information and its movement to long-term memory, teachers need to know that rehearsal and other strategies are required. As discussed under "Information Processing Model" (Lutz and Huitt 2003), moving information from short-term or working memory to long-term memory may involve rote or maintenance rehearsal, and more complex elaboration is required to transfer information to long-term memory. Lutz and Huitt (2003) indicated that "educators must ensure that new information is processed in such a way that it can be retained in long-term memory" (10). They noted that for this to occur, elaboration and connection need to take place between existing memory structures and new information. Elaborative rehearsal involves connecting new information with information already in long-term memory (Woolfolk 1998). Strategies that enhance retention in working memory and that facilitate transfer of information to long-term memory through encoding or linking new information with information already in long-term memory include rehearsal, both maintenance and more complex elaboration; chunking, which involves combining pieces of information to be processed as a single unit; and parallel use of verbal and spatial associations, or dual coding (Bonnema 2009).

Some additional strategies that facilitate moving information from short-term or working memory to long-term memory and that enhance long-term memory are suggested below:

- *Metacognitive Skill.* Kornell and Bjork (2009) indicated that in psychology, experts use the term *metacognition* to speak about how people think about their own cognitive processes or to think about thinking. They shared that managing one's own aspects of learning requires one to understand the activities involved and of the processes that best facilitate learning. Stanny (2009) indicated that metacognition involves knowledge of one's cognitive system and how it works. It is the ability to manage one's cognitive processes. In addition to metacognition, Stanny (2009) discussed metamemory and metacomprehension, closely related to metacognition. She defined *metamemory* as the ability to identify memory strategies that would apply to specific situations or content; to identify which strategies work best for learning; to evaluate the quality of one's own learning; to decide when one has studied sufficiently; to predict performance on a memory task; and to estimate the accuracy of retrieval. Stanny (2009) discussed *metacomprehension* as being able to monitor one's ability to understand instructions, explanations or other material that is read or heard; to determine when one's understanding is weak; and to identify and use strategies to correct one's misunderstandings. With regard to such self-regulation strategies, Stanny (2009) noted that learners must use feedback about their learning to alter and/or refine the strategies used, select and apply appropriate strategies, and determine the usefulness of the strategies selected. Accordingly, learners must know which strategies are available, how they work, and when they are most useful. Developing metacognitive skill is often recommended for enhancing problem solving/critical thinking (addressed in "Part 4—Problem-Solving-Type Learning").

- *Facilitating Active Involvement.* Other strategies facilitate students' active involvement in the learning process and thereby enhance memory. Such strategies may include clickers and computer-assisted instruction that permit students to receive immediate feedback on their learning as they engage in the learning process. Kagan (1992) suggested cooperative learning that lends itself to student interaction and participation. Also, cooperative learning may facilitate accountability for both individuals and groups. Cooperative learning strategies are suggested also in "Part 4—Problem-Solving-Type Learning: In Light of Recent Research."

Snow, Burns, and Griffen (1998) suggested reciprocal teaching/learning as a strategy to encourage active student involvement. This strategy uses summarizing, asking questions, making predictions, and clarifying content, as well as constructing meaning. Teachers and students take turns serving in the teacher role. In addition, simulations, role playing, debates, and projects can engage students in hands-on experiences and active learning (Banikowski and Mehring 1999).

In order to facilitate active involvement, teachers also need to include authentic learning activities (Bonnema 2009). Such activities may include projects, simulations, and problem-solving activities that are based on realistic problems/issues, such as those identified in one's local community. Authentic learning activities serve to enrich the learning environment, increase motivation for learning, and facilitate encoding of information.

- *Constructing Meaning.* Some strategies are designed to facilitate students' ability to construct meaning, as teachers help build background for what is to be learned and retained. In addition to the strategies focused on uncovering prior knowledge and building background, a strategy for constructing meaning involves use of a graphic organizer that represents abstract or implied information, shows relationships, helps organize ideas when linking new information with prior knowledge, and facilitates information storage and retrieval (Banikowski and Mehring 1999). Graphic organizers may include flowcharts, timelines, Venn diagrams, cause/effect diagrams, and story maps.

  In addition to graphic organizers, good strategies for constructing information are "outlining" strategies, used for organizing information in a way that identifies main points, their supporting details, important terms, and illustrations (Bogue 1993). She indicated that when taking notes from reading assignments, students using this strategy identify main points, supporting details and other items of information to be learned and make notes in a way that shows the relationship of ideas. Effectively taking notes from lectures/presentations requires students to organize the information in a way that helps construct meaning. Further, when marking written material, students who use an outlining strategy identify the major points and supporting details, key terms, and illustrations as they actively engage with the material, gain a clear sense of the content, and construct meaning.

  When preparing graphic organizers and notes from written material showing main points, supporting details, key terms, and reference to illustrations, students briefly write the points found in the material.

Such an activity requires students to think through the material and analyze it for major points and details. Ormrod (1998) suggested that the act of writing itself requires the brain to process information in a more in-depth manner.

Activating prior knowledge and facilitating students' integration of new ideas into memory, while linking those ideas with ideas already stored in long-term memory, as a means to construct knowledge or generate cognitive meanings, are addressed in "Part 4—Problem-Solving-Type Learning: In Light of Recent Research." Advance organizers are addressed as a means to facilitate problem solving / critical thinking.

- *Additional Strategies for Enhancing Memory.* Additional strategies that may be used to facilitate students' ability to retain information and demonstrate their learning are the following:

  - Bogue (1993) suggested several "test preparation" and "test taking" strategies that serve students well. In terms of test preparation, students should learn as much as possible about the test to be given, gather relevant material to study, organize it under main points and supporting details (if this step hasn't been taken), and recite material prior to taking the test, as doing so will help students remember and recall the information.
    Stanny (2009) also stressed the importance of self-testing. She suggested that students test themselves and complete self-constructed tests before taking a test administered by the teacher. Doing so enables students to determine their understanding of the material, review areas needing further study, and evaluate their ability to retrieve information.

    When taking tests and demonstrating what they have learned, students should read all test directions carefully and briefly survey the test before taking it. They should budget their time in order to complete all items and answer those they are sure of first. Also, they should quickly review answers before submitting the completed test (Bogue 1993).

☐ Stanny (2009) addressed the importance of distribution of practice, distinguishing between massed practice and distributed practice (spaced learning). Rohrer, Taylor, Pashler, Wixted, and Cepeda (2005) suggested a combination of drill and practice with distributed practice, as both can be useful to students. Stanny (2009) noted that when distributing study time, it is important to practice weaker items or content over short intervals in order to increase the strength of retrieval cues, using mass practice for initial learning. In addition, students should practice stronger items or content over increasingly long intervals, using distributed practice for items that have been partially learned.

☐ Further, Stanny (2009) recommended the use of mnemonics, including imagery mnemonics, chunking, which was discussed also by Bonnena (2009), hierarchical organizations, and acronyms, all of which may increase memory when used effectively.

When implementing strategies designed to enhance working memory and ultimately long-term memory, it is important to address individual learning needs of all students. In other words, to the extent possible, a teacher needs to differentiate instruction in order to respond to each student's needs. Sparapani (2013) noted that instruction needs to be student-centered and focused on students' ability levels and individual differences. While certain strategies to enhance memory and learning are recommended, it is important to remember that students come to the classroom with different levels of motivation to learn and ability to maintain focused attention. Students also have different levels of prior knowledge of numerous topics, habits of active engagement in the learning process, ability to construct meaning, and ability to demonstrate what they have learned. As a result of such differences, teachers are encouraged to consider implementing various instructional approaches and diversifying pedagogical strategies in order to meet student needs. Further, teachers should be aware of some factors that can impede learning, such as lack of sufficient sleep, poor nutrition, and high stress levels.

References for Part 2—Memory-Type Learning

Atkinson, R. C., and R. M. Shiffrin. 1968. "Human Memory: A Proposed System and Its Control Processes." In *The Psychology of Learning and Motivation Volume 2*, edited by K. W. Spence and J. T. Spence, 89–195. New York: NY: Academic Press.

Baddeley, A., and G. Hitch. 1974. "Working Memory." In *The Psychology of Learning and Motivation: Advances in Research and Theory, Volume 8*, edited by G. H. Bower, 47–89. New York, NY: Academic Press.

Baddeley, A. 2012. "Working Memory: Theories, Models, and Controversies." *Annual Review of Psychology* 63: 1–29.

Banikowski, A. K., and T. A. Mehring. 1999. "Strategies to Enhance Memory Based on Brain-Based Research." *Focus on Exceptional Children* 32, no. 2: 1–22.

Bogue, C. 1993. *Studying in the Content Areas: Social Science*. Clearwater, FL: H & H Publishing Co. Inc.

Bonnema, T. R. 2009. "Enhancing Student Learning with Brain-Based Research." Files.eric.ed.gov/fulltext/ED51009.pdf.

Craik, F. L. M., and R. S. Lockhart. 1972. "Levels of Processing: A Framework for Memory Research." *Journal of Verbal Learning and Verbal Behavior* 11: 671–684.

Eggen, P., and D. Kauchak. 1996. *Educational Psychology: Windows on Classrooms*. Columbus, OH: Merrill/Prentice Hall.

Huitt, W. 2003. "The Information Processing Approach to Cognition." *Educational Psychology Interactive*. Valdosta, GA: Valdosta State University. http://www.edpsycinteractive.org/topics/cognition/infoproc.html.

Kagan, S. 1992. *Cooperative Learning*. San Juan Capistrano, CA: Resources for Teachers, Inc.

Kornell, N., and R. A. Bjork. 2009. "A Stability Bias in Human Memory: Overestimating Remembering and Underestimating Learning." *Journal of Experimental Psychology: General* 138, no. 4: 449–468. doi.10.1037/a0017350.

Kuhara-Kojima, K., and G. Hatano. 1991. "Contribution of Content Knowledge and Learning Ability to the Learning of Facts." *Journal of Educational Psychology* 83, no. 2: 253–263.

Langer, J. A. 1981. "From Theory to Practice: A Prereading Plan." *Journal of Reading* 25: 152–156.

Langer, J. A. 1982. "Facilitating Text Processing: The Elaboration of Prior Knowledge." In *Reader Meets Author/Bridging the Gap: A Psycholinguistic and Sociolinguistic Perspective*, edited by J. A. Langer & M. T. Smith-Burke, 149–162. Newark, NJ: International Reading Association.

Lutz, S., and W. Huitt. 2003. "Information Processing and Meaning: Theory and Application." *Educational Psychology Interactive.* Valdosta, GA: Valdosta State University. www.edpsycinteractive.org/papers/infoproc.pdf.

McLeod, S. A. 2007a. "Multi Store Model of Memory." www.simplypsychology.org/multi-store.html.

McLeod, S. A. 2007b. "Levels of Processing." www.simplypsychology.org/levels of processing.html.

McLeod, S. A. 2008. "Information Processing." www.simplypsychology.org/information-processing.html.

McLeod, S. A. 2012. "Working Memory." www.simplypsychology.org/working%20memory.html.

Ormrod, J. E. 1998. *Educational Psychology: Developing Learners.* Columbus, OH: Merrill/Prentice Hall.

Qin, S., S. Cho, T. Chen, M. Rosenberg-Lee, D. C. Geary, and V. Menon. 2014. "Hippocampal-neocortical Functional Reorganization Underlies Children's Cognitive Development." *Nature Neuroscience* 17, no. 9 (September): 1263–1269. doi: 10.1038.nn.3788.

Rohrer, D., K. Taylor, H. Pashler, J. T. Wixted, and N. J. Cepeda. 2005. "The Effect of Overlearning on Long-Term Retention." *Applied Cognitive Psychology* 19: 361–374. ERIC Document Reproduction Service No. ED505637.

Slavin, R. E. 1997. *Educational Psychology: Theory and Practice.* Boston, MA: Allyn and Bacon.

Snow, C. E., M. S. Burns, and P. Griffen, eds. 1998. *Preventing Reading Difficulties in Young Children.* Washington, DC: National Academy Press.

Sparapani, E. F., ed. 2013. *Differentiated Instruction: Content Area Applications and Other Considerations for Teaching in Grades 5–12 in the Twenty-First Century.* Lanham, MD: University Press of America.

Stanny, C. J. 2009. *Memory Strategies and Metacognition.* Memory and Cognition Slide Presentation for EXP 4507. University of West Florida.

Woolfolk, A. E. 1998. *Educational Psychology.* Boston, MA: Allyn and Bacon.

PART 3

MOTOR-TYPE LEARNING: TIMELESS WISDOM

Introduction

The objectives or goals for motor learning focus on muscle movement, ranging from simple to complex. One may learn when relatively motionless, as when memorizing, reasoning, appreciating, or deriving percepts, but when movement and motion are incorporated, motor-type learning is involved. Motor skills require coordination of the brain, nervous system, and muscles and involve actions that require muscle movement. Gross motor skills involving large movements include walking, running, and jumping. Fine motor skills involve smaller actions, such as writing, drawing, playing musical instruments, planing boards, driving nails, handling apparatuses, or manipulating machines. Fine motor skills involve the use of the fingers, or toes, wrists, lips, or tongue. Many types of activities require both gross and fine motor skills. One should remember also that little knowledge and few skills are gained through only one type of learning. One or all four of the other types of learning may be used in acquiring motor skills.

Steps in the Acquisition of a Skill

For purposes of illustration, the following sequence describes the steps a learner should take in acquiring a fine motor skill of a somewhat simple nature. Also described are the steps that a teacher should take while directing the motor type of learning. The skill to be acquired is the ability to break glass tubing accurately, speedily, and safely.

- ❐ Initially, it is most important to build a mind-set for the motor skill or task to be learned. Frequently, a lesson involving motor type of learning is initiated by some remark from the teacher, such as, "Today I am going to show you how to break glass tubing." At this point, the teacher proceeds to demonstrate the task and does little to create a mind-set for the students. Building a real mind-set includes creating a desire within the pupils to want to know, to need to know, and to want to be able to do something. Consider a different approach by a truly outstanding elementary science teacher who shared the following with the class:

Anyone who is involved in science, particularly in the field of chemistry, uses apparatuses constantly in performing experiments. Glass tubing is frequently used as part of the apparatuses needed for this task. Our glass tubing comes in longer lengths than needed, so in our experiment today, it must be broken into desirable lengths. A good chemist learns to break glass tubing easily and accurately, and today we are going to take our time and try to become good chemists. Some children believe the way to break glass tubing is to grasp it and bend it until it breaks, just as one would break a crayon or a stick of candy. Glass tubing, however, cannot be broken so easily. Breaking glass tubing must be done properly or the tubing will not break evenly, and improper breaking may result in cuts. Do not put much faith in the glass; it acts in unexpected ways. It will act as you desire, however, if you treat it according to its nature. Would you like to know how to treat it so that the glass always breaks as you want it to break?

Using this approach to lead pupils to break glass tubing engages them and leads them to want to develop this skill. This approach for creating a mind-set produces in the learner a desire to acquire the skills involved, and it focuses attention on the remaining factors involved in this motor skill.

❐ After building a mind-set, the teacher must ensure that the pupils have a clear percept of the needed skill. Children cannot progress satisfactorily unless they have a clear picture of the end. The end, in this instance, includes the percept of the glass tubing when it is properly broken and the process/steps to follow in breaking it correctly. This excellent elementary science teacher proceeded by saying the following:

> The glass tubing, when well broken, is round and even. There are no jagged points, and there are no signs of cracks at the ends. To make the ideal break, one must file a small notch in the tubing, then clasp the tube with both hands, put the points of the thumbs together below the notch, and press downward and outward with the fingers and upward with the thumbs with an even pressure

until the tubing snaps apart. [Teacher demonstrates.] The notch weakens the tubing, and the tubing breaks evenly at the weakest spot. [Teacher draws figure on the chalkboard, showing how the thumbs are together and not spread apart.] If the thumbs aren't together, the pressure is not concentrated below the notch, and a poor break or cut may result.

The percept of the processes involved in this skill is developed through demonstration, graphic representations on the chalkboard, and verbal explanation. All three means produce a better percept than one would have without these steps. The graphic representations on the chalkboard are used to enlarge or emphasize details not easily gained in the demonstration or in a verbal explanation. Verbal explanations during demonstrations draw attention to the right sequence and/or to smaller details likely to be overlooked in observation. With the right percept clearly in mind, the children have an end in view that serves as a guide for the next steps in learning to break glass tubing.

❏ The third step involved in directing motor-type learning is ensuring correct initial performance. After the desire to break the tubing has been encouraged and the percept has been developed in the child's mind, the third step involves leading the child to make an initial attempt to perform the skill. During this step, correct performance must take precedence over speed or hasty execution. Children, as a rule, are generally inclined to plunge into a task at full steam ahead, forgetting and neglecting the essential steps that, when followed carefully, lead to smooth and efficient execution. Serving to illustrate this behavior, in the experiment with the glass tubing, some children filed a notch so deep that one would think they intended to file the tubing apart; some placed the notch on the underside of the tubing in making the break; and others held their thumbs flat against the tubing. While the children were trying to complete the tasks, their mistakes were detected, their difficulties analyzed, their oversights pointed out, and their percepts clarified and reinforced. No matter how slow the process, correct performance was not sacrificed for hasty execution. If poor procedures become firmly established, they will affect skill development. An inefficient and/or inaccurate way of doing things in the initial stages of performing a task requiring motor skill may certainly result in imperfect performance thereafter.

- ❐ The last step in directing motor-type learning involves providing for adequate practice for precision and/or speed of execution. When the correct initial performance has been demonstrated, that is, when the performance is satisfactory and correct processes for completing the task have been followed, the last step, involving repetition of the performance until it can be completed with precision and/or at the desired or appropriate rate of speed, can be taken. In breaking glass tubing, there is no particular need for speed because completing such a task should be done carefully and with precision. This skill is one that demands precision rather than performance speed. Many skills, however, need to be demonstrated at a desired rate of speed and are efficiently performed only after much repetition, involving hours and hours of practice, extending over weeks and even months.

The four steps in motor learning, although applied to a relatively simple skill, hold equally well in the learning of any motor skill. There are, however, psychological factors of which teachers must be aware. Such factors confront teachers who are responsible for leading students to develop some complicated skills—skills requiring more time, direction, and precision in learning. Some of these skills, to be effectively understood and taught, demand more extensive treatment than can be described in this writing on motor-type learning.

A few related general principles for directing motor learning, which are closely related to the steps mentioned thus far, are described below:

- ❐ One principle focuses on learning motor skills as a whole versus breaking the skill into parts. When should the skill be learned as a whole? When should the parts be learned by themselves first and then joined together in order to demonstrate the whole skill? As a general rule, skills that are not too complex should be learned as a whole. For example, in learning to write, it is better to write the whole word(s) than to practice making a whole series of *n*'s, *a*'s, followed by *t*'s, and so forth. Doing so reinforces visual discrimination, pronunciation, and spelling and at the same time perfects handwriting skill.

For more complex skills, such as learning to type or to swim, the skill cannot be learned as a whole and should be broken into parts. Even in such cases, however, the parts should be combined in practice so that skills gradually approximate a higher level/stage and finally result in the complete act. In other words, the parts must not remain separate skills but should be welded together as soon as possible into a closer approximation of the end in view, until the end itself is attained.

❏ Teachers should use true-to-life conditions for addressing and monitoring correct initial performance and when conducting practice for speed of execution. For example, writing, as performed in daily living, is done with a pencil or pen. The material used to write upon is paper, ruled or unruled. There are no models to follow except the images in one's mind. No one will be available to guide the hand if it cannot make the letter formations. These conditions are the ones under which writing proceeds in actual life. At one time, many years ago, in our schools, a *groove board* was used—a board with capital and small letters perfectly grooved upon it. The child was asked to take some pointed instrument and follow the groove, with the intent to give the muscles and fingers the feel of perfect letters.

After this exercise, the pupil, it was thought, would be able to make good letters in actual writing with a pen or pencil upon paper. This practice, however, was discontinued because it was inefficient, and it was inefficient because it did not provide training in the way writing is truly carried out in real-life situations. The same applies to other activities requiring motor skill. If one is big enough, strong enough, and old enough to learn to ride a bicycle, then the person should practice with a real bicycle. If one is mature enough to learn to swim, water is the medium in which to learn this activity. This principle that stresses practice under true-to-life conditions is very important.

❏ After the desired initial-performance level has been demonstrated, and the child continues to practice for speed of execution, the question of length of practice periods and their distribution must be considered. No hard-and-fast specifications can be established in answer to this question because children vary in their ability to learn motor skills, and skills vary in their demand upon children. Some skills require little exertion and little attention during practice, while others require much exertion and constant strain upon the muscles and mind. Experimental evidence seems to indicate that for learning most motor skills, daily practice periods of specified amounts of time (and sometimes two practice periods properly distributed during the same day) will yield best results. The evidence, in short, shows that daily practice periods of the right length, distributed over a period of time (days, weeks, or months) produce better learning of motor skills than long periods scheduled in a short period of time. For example, it has been shown, as one might expect, that after fifteen to thirty minutes of intense application, a pupil reaches a point where fatigue, interest and strain inhibit or impede further improvement. It is only when pupils are able to devote their best efforts that real improvement can be made. When individuals are dawdling, uninterested, or just putting in time, they will not make much progress in learning a motor skill. Practice should be periods of intense activity, during which the learners are working at their best. At the point in practice when learners cannot remain at their best, there should be a rest period. It is better to strive for higher and higher levels of performance through one's very best efforts than to remain at the same level or regress to lower levels of execution due to stressful and monotonous repetition.

In general, the length of the practice periods should be based on the principle of working up to one's maximum potential while practicing. The number of practice sessions generally should be one or two a day, over a length of time sufficient to reach the desired goal.

As noted earlier, more complex motor learning, to a large extent, is confined to learning particular kinds of tasks, so a more exhaustive treatment of this topic is required. Such treatment will not be undertaken in this writing. General classroom teachers might consult with teachers of specialized areas where motor skill development is an essential part of the program, such as physical education, art, and music. Teachers in these areas stress motor learning in its intensive and extensive application.

Application Exercises

- Percepts play an important part in motor learning. Give several illustrations.
- In a social studies lesson at the sixth-grade level, the teacher wrote major points on the chalkboard. One point was "Explain what 'Cotton is king' meant to the people in the South." One pupil interpreted the quoted sentence as "Cottou is king." He said he didn't know the man. The teacher had made the N look like a U. Analyze your own penmanship, and determine its quality. Watch for any closed *e*'s, uncrossed *t*'s, *m*'s that look like *u*'s, *n*'s that resemble *u*'s, *cl*'s that look like *d*'s, spacing between letters, unevenness of letters, and the different slants of various letters.
- Years ago educators placed considerable emphasis upon best methods in learning skills. The child's pencil was to be held in a certain position, the batter was to stand at the plate in a specified way, and the grip on the bat was to be just so. Although best methods may no longer be given as much consideration, there are still some best ways of learning motor skills. Are there best methods in holding a pencil? Positions while playing musical instruments? Explain why a cross-handed batter will never be a sure and powerful hitter in baseball. Why does knowing how to walk a straight line aid one in the reading process? How does ability in patting one's head and rubbing one's stomach simultaneously aid a person in performing two activities at the same time?

PART 3

MOTOR-TYPE LEARNING: IN LIGHT OF RECENT RESEARCH

Introduction

Current literature contains much information regarding motor behavior. As summarized in *Introduction to Motor Development, Control, and Motor Learning* (n.d.), motor behavior consists of three major aspects:

- ☐ Motor development that examines the underlying processes of motor behavior and changes in human motor behavior through one's life time. Motor development also refers to the factors that affect these changes.
- ☐ Motor learning that emphasizes the process involved in acquiring motor skill and the factors that affect performance of a motor skill.
- ☐ Motor control that focuses on neural, physical, and behavioral aspects of human movement and how the neuromuscular system serves to set in motion and coordinate muscles and limbs used in skill performance.

Focus herein will be placed on the learning of motor skills and instructional strategies that facilitate their acquisition.

Definition

According to Newell (1991), "The study of motor skill acquisition is viewed as distinct from the study of the related subdomains of motor control and motor development" (213). He noted that motor control refers to the control of movement, whereas motor development refers to the children's motor skills and focuses on the sequence of events that occur in the development of a specific group of organisms. He indicated:

> Motor skill acquisition originated as a branch of experimental psychology and was labeled accordingly as opposed to verbal learning, which is what it had been called. Motor skill acquisition is distinguished from motor control, which originated in physiology, and represents the neurophysiology of the motor system. (214)

Newell (1991) also noted that motor skill usually refers to those skills in which both the movement and outcome of action are emphasized. According to Wilmerding and Krasnow (2009), there are several stages essential to the motor learning process, including attention and observation or perception of a demonstrated skill (dependent on the senses: sight, touch, taste, smell and hearing), replication or carrying out the observed skill, feedback or knowledge of results or performance, and repetition or additional practice.

Schmidt and Lee (2011) defined motor learning as "a set of internal processes associated with practice or experience leading to relatively permanent changes in the capability for motor skill" (497). Schmidt and Wrisberg (2008) noted, "Motor learning is an internal process or state, the level of which reflects a person's capability for producing a movement at any particular point in time" (21). In this sense, then, motor learning refers to those internal processes that are linked to experience or practice and that lead to relatively permanent changes in ability to produce a motor skill. Wilmerding and Krasnow (2009) noted that while the result of motor learning is permanent, the motor system is capable of change throughout one's life.

In terms of motor skills, a distinction is made between gross motor skills and fine motor skills. Gross motor skills involve movement related to large muscles and coordination of arms, legs, and other body parts and movements. For example, running, jumping, and throwing are considered gross motor skills. Fine motor skills involve smaller muscle groups and require more precise movements, typically involving hand-eye coordination. Fine motor skills involve small movements in wrists, fingers, hands, fists, and toes. Examples of fine motor skills are writing, buttoning a blouse, playing a musical instrument, and using a brush and watercolors to paint a picture (Einon n.d.). Einon pointed out that in any area of a baby's body, gross motor skills develop prior to fine motor skills. For example, children learn how to bring their arms together before passing a favorite toy from one hand to another.

Newell (1991) noted that motor skills are usually distinguished from perceptual, cognitive, communication, and other skill categories, but he noted that "traditional distinctions have been made primarily for heuristic convenience. As a consequence, skill categories reflect primarily differences in scholarly emphasis rather than mutually exclusive avenues of scholarly inquiry" (214).

Classroom Application

In today's schools it is important to address motor learning, beginning with fundamental motor skills, such as running, leaping, and catching, as these skills provide the foundation for learning more complex movement skills. Mastery of these skills is required for the development of more complex skills, and their refinement is very important to children in school. As indicated in the Department of Education, Victoria, 1996 publication, *Fundamental Motor Skills: A Manual for Classroom Teachers,* the level of competence in motor skills affects students in many ways, including their self-perception, social acceptance, and positive attitude toward physical activity. Many educators concur that physical activity contributes to children's physical and mental health, social and emotional skills, and academic achievement. In general, competence in basic or fundamental motor skills helps students prepare for a healthy and enriched lifestyle.

Strategies to Develop Motor Skill

In discussing the steps involved with acquiring motor skill, Carline addressed the need to develop a mind-set, which referred to the need to increase student understanding of the activity involved and to create a desire to do something and the need to know something. In recent literature, we find much emphasis placed on the degree to which cognitive elements (or knowing what to do) and motor elements (or knowing how to do it) contribute to achieving a motor skill or reaching a desired performance level (Schmidt and Wrisberg 2008).

As Wilmerding and Krasnow (2009) indicated, teachers should understand several aspects of motor learning and implement appropriate strategies in order to create an environment conducive to learning motor skills. They noted that the process of motor learning begins with attention and perception, and they shared that in order to teach motor skills, teachers typically demonstrate the skill to be learned while the students observe and attach meaning to what they see, based on past experience. Further, they noted that the teacher's goal should be to work with the students and help them fine-tune the skills that they already have. In addition, teachers should identify the children's learning abilities and preferences in order to select approaches for presenting or demonstrating the skills (Wilmerding and Krasnow 2009).

While motor learning is initiated by perception, children master a skill with replication and repetition. In order to accommodate the need for repetition, different practice schedules (massed or distributed schedules) need to be considered. Haibach, Reid, and Collier (2011) noted that the type of task should be matched with the most appropriate practice schedule. Massed practice, which involves fewer but longer practice sessions, more practice trials per session, and short rest periods between trials, is considered effective for discrete skills such as hitting a golf ball. Distributed practice, however, which involves more but shorter practice sessions, fewer practice trials per session, and longer rest intervals, is appropriate for continuous skills such as swimming and dancing.

Wilmerding and Krasnow (2009) noted that during the scheduled practice sessions, learning a movement is dependent on how information is presented, whether visually through skill demonstration, verbally through explanation of the process and proper execution of the skill, and/or kinesthetically through use of hands-on touch and/or assistance for clarification.

Wilmerding and Krasnow (2009) also indicated that following the teacher's demonstration and the students' initial attempts at completing the task, teachers should provide students feedback or information regarding how they executed the movement. It is well known that feedback is very important in the motor learning process. When the student executes the movement accurately and efficiently, the accurate movement patterns become part of the long-term or habitual memory. If the student practices the movement incorrectly, the incorrect movement becomes ingrained. Teachers, therefore, need to provide verbal, visual, and/or kinesthetic feedback without delay when the student is learning a new motor skill. When providing feedback, teachers need to be supportive and point out positive aspects of execution when addressing the areas that need improvement (Wilmerding and Krasnow 2009).

Haibach, Reid, and Collier (2011) stressed the importance of structuring a learning environment that addresses motivation and that is conducive to initiating an activity, repeating it, and persisting in its execution. They indicated that an environment that is conducive to learning reflects much encouragement, goal setting, social interactions, mastery, and positive feedback. Teachers should advise students what aspect of the movement or skill needs improvement and what is being executed appropriately and efficiently. As Carline noted, at the initial stage of presenting particular motor skills, teachers need to provide feedback and correction at the start. With complex motor skills, it is also important to address the appropriate form in the initial stages. The appropriate form provides the foundation for the skills to be developed. Also, as we read in *How Children Learn Motor Skills* (2015), teachers of complex motor skills, such as golf, tennis, and skiing, often must lead students to take a step backward, unlearn their current techniques, and replace them with accurate ones. Repeated practice of the proper technique then leads to mastery of the motor skill.

Sullivan, Kantak, and Burtner (2008) reported on a study that drew conclusions about providing feedback during motor learning, noting that in contrast to adults, children who were provided reduced feedback during practice performed with less accuracy and consistency during the retention test than those who were provided 100 percent feedback. However, when feedback was reintroduced during the reacquisition test, the children in the reduced feedback group did improve their performance comparable to those in the 100 percent feedback group. A conclusion reached in the study was that when learning a motor skill, children use feedback in a different way than adults to achieve motor learning goals. Children may require that feedback be reduced more gradually, as compared with young adults, and children may require longer practice periods.

Teachers also need to establish goals for the students and thereby motivate them to persist in repetition. Considerable repetition is needed, especially for complex motor skills. Further, Haibach et al. (2011) warned that rewards should be used wisely in order to maintain high levels of intrinsic motivation.

Whole versus Part Instruction

Carline indicated that motor skills that are not too complex should be learned as a whole. He shared also that more complicated skills may need to be broken into parts and combined in practice so that an approximation of the complete motor skill can be gradually attained. Nixon and Locke (1973) indicated as well that ideally, motor skills should be taught as a whole. They noted that when the skill is complex, the teacher may need to break down the complex movement into its parts and then link those parts to develop the final skill. For complex skills, they suggested a whole-part-whole instructional strategy, when the student attempts the whole skill while the teacher identifies those parts that the student executes improperly. Part instruction is then used to address the problem areas, after which the student repeats the whole skill. Others, including Schmidt and Lee (2005) and Weitl (2010) also indicated preference for whole training, as opposed to part training for motor skill acquisition.

References for Part 3—Motor-Type Learning

Department of Education, Victoria. 1996. *Fundamental Motor Skills: A Manual for Classroom Teachers.* Melbourne Vic 3001, Australia: Community Information Service.

Einon, D. n.d. "What's the Difference between Fine Motor and Gross Motor Skills?" www.babycentre.co.uk/x6562/whats-the-difference between-fine-motor-and-gross-motor-skills.

Haibach, P. S., G. Reid, and D. H. Collier. 2011. *Motor Learning and Development.* Champaign, IL: Human Kinetics Publishers.

"How Children Learn Motor Skills." 2015. *Great Play: Interactive Gym for Kids.* www.greatplay.com/articles/how-children-learn-motor-skills.

"Introduction to Motor Development, Control, and Motor Learning." n.d. www.d.umn.edu~dmillsla/courses/motorlearning/documents/ Introduction to Motor Development.pdf.

Newell, K. M. 1991. "Motor Skill Acquisition." *Annual Review of Psychology* 42 (February): 213–237. doi: 10.1146/annurev.ps.42.020191.001241.

Nixon, J. E., and L. F. Locke. 1973. "Research on Teaching Physical Education." In *Second Handbook of Research on Teaching*, edited by R. M. W. Travers, 1210–1242. Chicago, IL: Rand McNally & Co.

Schmidt. R. A., and T. D. Lee. 2005. *Motor Control and Learning: A Behavioral Emphasis.* Champaign, IL: Human Kinetics Publishers.

Schmidt. R. A., and T. D. Lee. 2011. *Motor Control and Learning: A Behavioral Emphasis.* Champaign, IL: Human Kinetics Publishers.

Schmidt, R. A. and C. A. Wrisberg. 2008. *Motor Learning and Performance: A Situation-Based Learning Approach.* Champaign, IL: Human Kinetics Publishers.

Sullivan, K. J., S. S. Kantak, and P. A. Burtner. 2008. "Motor Learning in Children: Feedback Effects on Skill Acquisition." *Physical Therapy* 88, no. 6: 720–732.

Weitl, D. 2010. "Whole vs. Part Training." *Coaching Volleyball* 27, no. 3: 8–11.

Wilmerding, V., and D. Krasnow. 2009. "Motor Learning and Teaching Dance." Resource paper for the International Association for Dance Medicine and Science. www.iadms.org/displaycommon.cfm?an=1&subarticlenbr=186.

PART 4

PROBLEM-SOLVING-TYPE LEARNING: TIMELESS WISDOM

Introduction

Keeping in mind the aforementioned types of learning and their focused learning activities, consider now the nature of the problem-solving type of learning and related activities. It is important to understand the kind of skills involved with problem solving and evaluate one's learning in this regard. Do you have the ability at this time to change Fahrenheit degrees to Celsius degrees and vice versa without formulas as props? If 8 is 35% of a number, what is the number? Of course, you must be the judge of your own performance level when answering these questions. If you really understood how to resolve such problems at some time in the past, you thought them through, and your analysis became part of you. If now you must revert to some memorized formula or try to juggle the words or figures to get the answers, you probably did not understand how to solve such problems originally. How does it happen that some persons have real mastery of what they initially learn while others do not? There must have been a difference somewhere in the individuals' learning, and the difference, no doubt, could be attributed to the activities employed during the learning process. At any rate, when genuine understanding is the goal, activities used to facilitate appropriate levels of understanding can best be called "reasoning activities." On the contrary, if one's goal is to repeat words or to manipulate formulas mechanically, one can achieve the goal by rote or verbatim learning, but what progress would be made if real and lasting comprehension were the goal?

Importance of Reasoning

During a lifetime, one must address many problems in one way or another. One can resolve a problem by accepting a solution worked out by someone else, or one can solve or attempt to solve the problem through one's own efforts. Textbooks give information that children memorize verbatim; some children work slavishly to memorize the thoughts or solutions described by others. Perhaps a day will come when the textbook will not provide all the worked-out statements. Rather, students will need to arrive at solutions independently and analyze them in light of solutions offered by others. Having an opportunity to learn and practice reasoning skills is of great value to all students, not only when in school but throughout life. Without such opportunities and practice, students can become deeply discouraged and unable to think through their own problems and difficulties in life that need to be addressed through critical thinking.

In your own experience, can you identify the difference between actually solving a problem and memorizing a rule or formula to solve the problem? Which resulted in mastery? In which case did you really learn and experience new insights? In which case was retention long lasting? In which case did you grow intellectually stronger and more independent? The same will be true for your pupils.

Types of Reasoning

Throughout all grade levels, teachers need to address two types of reasoning, both of which are complementary. The first is inductive reasoning, which fosters thinking by moving from specific to general ideas. The word *inductive* refers to impelling, moving, promoting, stirring up, and/or causing and means to continuously add more detail and specific facts that bind together and form a generalization. Inductive reasoning makes broad generalizations from specific observations/details, and it proceeds from the specific to the general. This type of reasoning may be referred to as *bottom-up logic.*

Deductive reasoning is the opposite of inductive reasoning and may draw upon one's experiential background or stored generalization to address a particular situation. In other words, deductive reasoning means continuously deducting one fact or idea from a generalization until one reaches a single or specific idea. According to dictionary definitions, deductive reasoning is a logical process wherein a conclusion or statement is based on multiple premises that are generally assumed to be true, or moving from the general to the more specific. Deductive reasoning may be referred to as *top-down logic.* The following testimony of a sixth-grade student illustrates the complementary nature of the two kinds of reasoning:

> My teacher is teaching us the parts of speech. We have learned nouns, pronouns, verbs, and adverbs. She told me to memorize them, which means to repeat their definitions over and over again in my mind so that I can learn them. Two days later, I couldn't give the definitions. Other pupils in the class couldn't either, so the teacher kept us after school. We

worked for forty minutes after school, and we memorized the definitions very well. The next morning when I went to school and the teacher asked us if we knew the definitions, about three-fourths of the class couldn't remember them. Despite the forty-minute study time after school the night before, our memorized work slipped away into the night, so we were told to take our books home every night that week and to memorize the definitions each night because the teacher didn't dare have another lesson with us if one single person made it a poor lesson.

Memory activities have a place in the learning process, but they are not good ones to set in motion when development of reasoning skills is at stake. In learning those parts of speech, for example, inductive reasoning should have been used in building up generalizations, and generalizations in this case would be the definitions. On the contrary, the sixth-graders attempted to memorize the generalizations (definitions) without knowing the meaning of what they were memorizing. As soon as the youngsters tried to determine the part of speech of a word in a sentence, they began to reason deductively.

There is no advantage, however, in making a sharp distinction between the two types of reasoning. If teachers realize fully the nature of the learning goal, they will direct learning so that the necessary activities, whether inductive or deductive or both, are set in motion. Further, we can say that sound thinking involves implementing activities related to both inductive and deductive reasoning, which are always employed together. On the other hand, if teachers are not concerned with deep understandings, insights, applications, and development of problem-solving skills but are satisfied with bare repetition of words, they will surely revert to rote memorization activities in guiding learning. Unless truly interested in problem solving/critical thinking and reasoning skills, teachers likely will show little concern for implementing activities that underlie their attainment.

Those teachers who espouse development of reasoning skills should design problem-solving activities that lead to utmost self-discovery through maximum individual effort. I use the words *maximum individual effort* to signify that while assisting pupils in various ways and at different times, teachers should not do so much that pupils resort to passive memorization of ideas and thoughts of another. Teachers should stimulate and lead pupils to self-discovery of ideas through pupils' maximum individual effort.

Reasoning and Nonreasoning Activities

At this point, it is necessary to further examine the difference between problem-solving skills and the memorization and retention of another's ideas. Often the latter are mistaken for reasoning. In reality, however, they involve activities that fall under memory or other type of learning. In a social studies test under the heading of "Problems," we see the following: "How did this country come to be discovered? How were the colonies settled? How did the people live? What is the story of the tariff? What is the history of our present Constitution?" Do these questions require problem solving? In all seriousness, probably not one of these questions requires problem-solving skills to provide a response. Answers to such questions can be found by reading a few pages in the textbook. Using information prepared by another to answer such questions can be accomplished by reading and remembering what is read. It is desirable that one should know much about how our country came to be discovered, but such a question does not demand reasoning skills to provide the answer. Suppose you visit a sixth-grade classroom and hear the teacher say, "We have just finished our problem. What is the history of our present Constitution?" Would you think that reasoning skills are required to provide the answer? Was there a problem to be solved?

To frame questions requiring reasoning skills to arrive at answers/conclusions, consider the following sequence. Let's say that you ask the pupils, "What did the men at the convention do about the number of senators from each state?"

Every hand goes up, and you ask Mary to share the answer. Mary says, "There was a compromise, and it was settled by having two senators from each state."

As of yet, it doesn't appear that Mary or any of the other pupils has needed to apply reasoning skills because the fact representing the answer is boldly stated in the textbook.

Next you ask, "Which states supported having the same number of senators from each state?"

Merely three hands go up this time, and the answers are *New York*, *Virginia*, and *Massachusetts*. Guessing is in progress. Students have encountered these states more frequently in the textbook than other states.

Now you tell the pupils that the textbook says that the small states steadfastly supported two senators from each state. Then you ask, "Why did the small states insist that there be two senators from each state?"

This time there is not a hand up. The faces are almost blank. These pupils did well in remembering textbook information, but reading a textbook is not problem solving. The answer to the last question is not in the textbook.

In order to help these pupils, the teacher needs to recognize that this situation requires reasoning, and this is an opportunity to lead students to self-discovery through maximum individual effort. At this point, students must employ problem-solving and reasoning activities to answer the question. There is no alternative.

John Dewey (1910), the education pragmatist, said it in this way:

> We may recapitulate by saying that the origin of thinking is some perplexity, confusion or doubt. Thinking is not a case of spontaneous combustion; it does not occur just on "general principles." There is something specific which occasions and evokes it. General appeals to a child (or to a grown-up) to think, irrespective of the existence in his own experience of his own difficulty that troubles him and disturbs his equilibrium, are as futile as advice to lift himself by his boot-straps. (12)

Problem solving done in school is prompted by specific questions/projects related to topics studied. Calling a topic a problem to solve is inaccurate if reasoning skills are not required to respond to the questions or to complete relevant projects. Responding to some questions may require pupils to draw upon memory, sensory experience, motor learning, and emotional learning but not necessarily problem-solving-type learning. In order to respond to questions that do require problem-solving/reasoning skills, pupils studying the topic need to build up background information and accumulate relevant facts, skills, and ideas gained by several types of learning and then apply the problem-solving/reasoning skills that are required to solve the problems or complete the projects.

In addition to raising questions that require pupils' reasoning skills, teachers also need to set the stage for requiring application of problem-solving/reasoning skills and lead pupils to arrive at solutions and/or reach conclusions independently. It can be viewed as the teacher's duty to arrange for situations or activities that require pupils to reason by themselves. Indeed, good teaching is entitled to be called "good" when it includes good goals and utilizes good procedures. Among the procedures that should be used are those that promote independence and self-discovery in problem solving / critical thinking through maximum individual effort.

Opportunities in Teaching to Promote Reasoning

An alert teacher constantly watches for problem-solving opportunities to present to the students. Such a teacher uses problems that, when solved, will reflect improved reasoning skill and clarification of ideas. In any given assignment, during questioning, during class discussion, in developmental procedures, in introducing new vocabulary, in organizing new work/projects, and in arranging self-learning activities, there are abundant opportunities to frame questions and to design projects that require problem-solving/reasoning skills. Further, when designing problem-solving questions, tasks, or projects, a teacher needs to have specific objectives and the learning environment in mind.

Environment for Instilling a Love of Reading, Learning, and Reasoning

Earl C. Kelley (1969), in *Humanizing the Education of Children*, stated that humanizing the education of children comes down to a question of adult values. If we cherish people above things, we will behave in a way consistent with that value. If we care more about the arithmetic problem than we do for the inner feelings of the child learning to solve the problem, we will then behave in a very different way. Many children fail to learn to think and apply good reasoning skills because the educational environment has been dehumanized. Such an environment doesn't permit children the opportunity to become involved in thinking and reasoning. Our schools as they are organized today, with all of their innovations and multistaff arrangements, often place too little emphasis on development of thinking and reasoning. With the aim of education crying for a full and deep development of critical-thinking skills, a teacher cannot rest easy or be content with the soft "hearing of the lessons" as the whole of teaching. The importance of developing critical thinkers is clearly underscored in the literature.

In today's schools, however, we often see too much emphasis placed on the impression and too little on designing the right kinds of activities for pupils. As mentioned, Dr. Kelly indicated that if we cherish people above things, we will behave in a way consistent with that value. The emphasis in our schools needs to be on appropriate activities designed for the classroom rather than on the impression.

Given this reality, learners are given insufficient opportunity to think and reason for themselves. Further, our curricula are composed of materials that are remote from the learners and, in some cases, of little interest to them. As a result, these learners have no great desire to think. In addition, our learners are told or made to feel that their opinions are not valued. The message they receive is that they should follow, not lead; listen and remember, not work things out for themselves. Many teachers have insufficient knowledge concerning the learning process, the nature of the child, and principles of child development. As a result, teachers often fail to give the type of direction needed to require their pupils to learn how to think. The problems assigned are too often ill-adapted to the child's capacity and experiences.

To create an environment conducive to real learning, teachers must understand children's capacity to think and then provide activities that lead them to reach their full potential. With this in mind, teachers need to be conscious of the learning goals that they establish. In light of these goals and objectives, they can better design problem-solving questions, tasks, and projects. The objectives should be twofold: focus on knowledge to be learned, and focus on thinking/reasoning skills and other closely related skills to be developed.

In addition, teachers need to plan the frequency of problem-solving activities and assess the quality of their students' thinking as they undertake assigned tasks. Teachers should not be relegated to the role of "clerk" but must engage students in the whole learning process and monitor their engagement. Following assessment, teachers need to provide direction and assign work that will help pupils overcome deficiencies in specific areas of problem solving / critical thinking.

Unless such conditions are arranged, monitored, and maintained, pupils may not learn how to think constructively while completing assigned tasks. Children who have not been taught how to think accurately and constructively are children *who have failed to learn how to learn from books.* Children who do not know how to learn from books have the most serious reading and learning problems in the nation today. In fact, the greatest problem in achieving appropriate levels of reading performance and learning in our schools is *not* that children are not learning how to read words—they are learning word analysis skills involved in reading and are taught to read words accurately. The greatest problem is that they have not been taught how to think. As a result, they do not know how to learn from books, and therefore many children refuse to read.

- One suggested practice for instilling in children a love of reading and learning—and ultimately problem solving / critical thinking—is Uninterrupted Sustained Silent Reading. The highest priority for increasing children's love of reading is to give them the opportunity to practice the reading processes that they have been taught. Children often have insufficient opportunity to practice what they have been taught simply because the teachers take up all the practice time with teaching. A basic commitment for developing readers is to first of all establish a reading environment. There must be a specific time of the day when reading will be looked upon as the most important part of the child's day in school. The specified time will enable the young minds to "sort things out," to understand what they are doing, and to see the purpose in their learning environment. They must not be hurried; they must not be expected to perform a lesson a day but only permitted to practice and internalize that which has been taught during reading instruction. Children will benefit greatly if they are allowed time to really understand and assimilate, indirectly and informally, at their own pace and in their own capacity, the fundamental aspects of the reading process. The mandate for Uninterrupted Sustained Silent Reading is as follows:

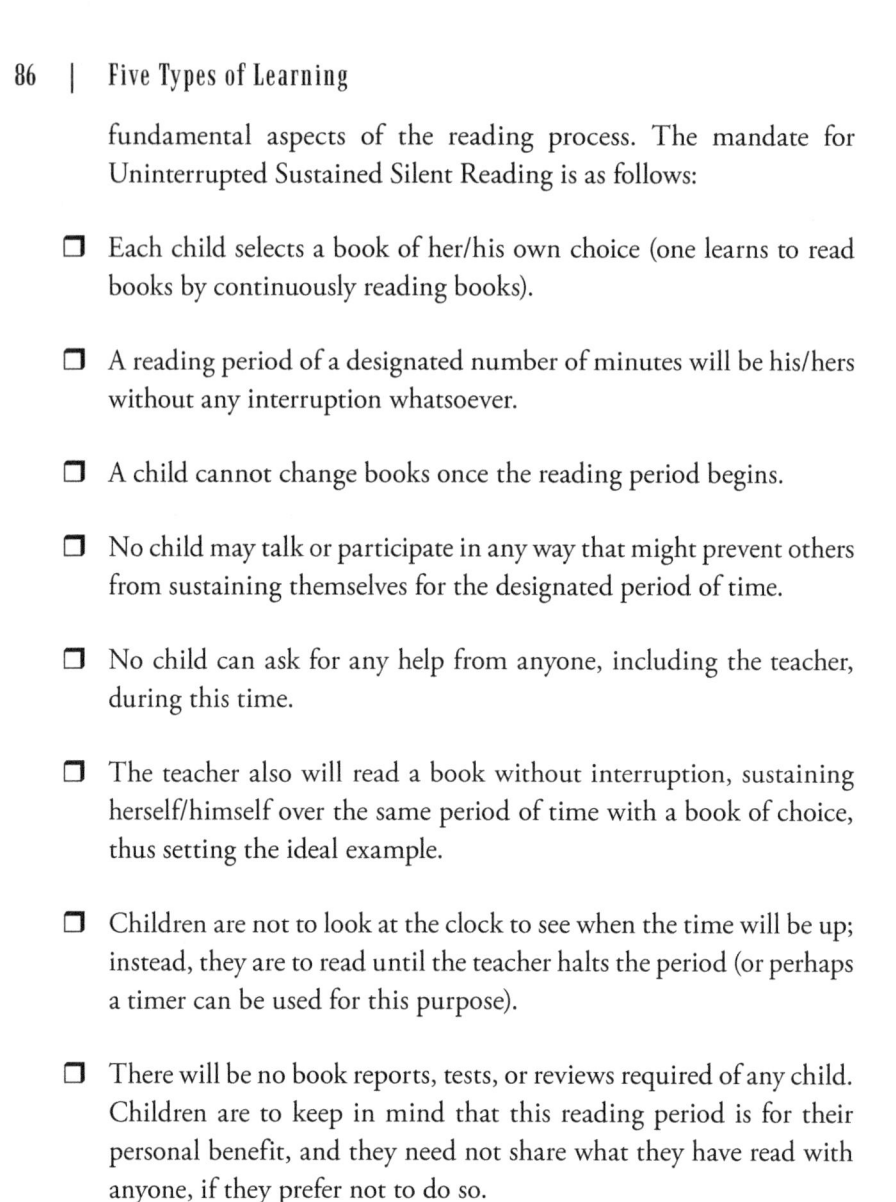

- ❏ Each child selects a book of her/his own choice (one learns to read books by continuously reading books).

- ❏ A reading period of a designated number of minutes will be his/hers without any interruption whatsoever.

- ❏ A child cannot change books once the reading period begins.

- ❏ No child may talk or participate in any way that might prevent others from sustaining themselves for the designated period of time.

- ❏ No child can ask for any help from anyone, including the teacher, during this time.

- ❏ The teacher also will read a book without interruption, sustaining herself/himself over the same period of time with a book of choice, thus setting the ideal example.

- ❏ Children are not to look at the clock to see when the time will be up; instead, they are to read until the teacher halts the period (or perhaps a timer can be used for this purpose).

- ❏ There will be no book reports, tests, or reviews required of any child. Children are to keep in mind that this reading period is for their personal benefit, and they need not share what they have read with anyone, if they prefer not to do so.

With this activity, reading gradually becomes a process of interaction between child and book. The interaction is so great that at times the children may feel that they are having an internal dialogue with the author. As a result, the time allotted to Uninterrupted Sustained Silent Reading can be lengthened as children become more interested in the reading material and likewise more proficient in reading. As children gain proficiency in reading, teachers can lead them to become more adept in learning and in applying problem-solving/critical-thinking skills.

Practical Guidelines for Teaching Children to Think

In addition to increasing reading and thinking skills through high-quality instruction and Uninterrupted Sustained Silent Reading, the following list summarizes main points for teaching problem solving / critical thinking and provides additional suggestions that will prove helpful when teachers and parents assist children in developing these skills.

- ❐ The teacher should provide problems that are well adapted to the children's ability levels, to their background experiences, and to their present motivation to succeed.

- ❐ The teacher should refrain from providing too much of the response when asking children to apply reasoning/critical-thinking skills. If the teacher does so, the learning process will be jeopardized, and children will not effectively apply critical-thinking skills.

- ❐ Teachers and parents should answer carefully and sympathetically every question asked by a child and in a way that will stimulate further thinking. They should not discourage thought by making light of questions asked or by treating the questions as insignificant. A question that seems ridiculous or useless to an adult may be very significant to a child.

- ❐ Children must be allowed to investigate things for themselves and should be encouraged to do so. Exploratory learning helps children practice reasoning/thinking skills.

- ❐ Teachers should arrange instruction to stimulate learners to gather numerous facts that will provide perceptual experiences and serve as the foundation for related problem-solving/critical-thinking tasks. Doing so also motivates children to continue studying and reading.

Knowing that they are learning something when engaged with printed material provides children incentive to learn.

- ❐ The directions for the problem to be solved must be clearly understood by all learners.

- ❐ Teachers should guide learners in organizing their ideas and drawing conclusions that will help inform analysis of material presented.

- ❐ Teachers should pay special attention to checking the learners' thoughts and work. Formative assessment is crucial to development of reasoning/critical-thinking skills. This process verifies the relevance of the learners' thinking to the problem to be solved.

- ❐ Teachers should lead learners to test the results of their independent thinking, so important to the formative assessment process, and lead them to develop the habit of supporting each important conclusion with explicitly stated supporting facts (i.e., the facts that are used to reach the conclusion).

- ❐ Teachers should guide learners in analyzing and solving parts of the problem presented so that learners can identify and resolve more significant parts of the problem.

- ❐ The problem assigned must be of interest to the learner. Otherwise, the learner may make little progress in reasoning and thinking critically.

- ❐ Teachers should remember that children's attempts at critical thinking may appear trivial at first, but eventually children will demonstrate effective habits of critical thinking. Ineffective attempts at critical thinking are especially evident when learners have little experience with the kind or type of problem presented and little experience with the material/content.

Development of Personal Attributes: A Real Value

By this time, you should understand, from your own experience and self-analysis, the importance of growth in personal attributes as an aim in school learning. Growth in personal attributes does not come without nourishment, and it must be nourished by appropriate opportunities. Some personal attributes are developed as part of the problem-solving/critical-thinking process. As teachers lead students to solve problems, they need to stress the importance, for example, of suspending judgment until all of the evidence has been brought to bear upon the problem. In itself, suspending judgment is a personal attribute that we admire in others and that is found in a person who weighs the evidence, a person who is somewhat critical, a person who does not believe everything read and heard, and a person who avoids biased thinking. While suspending judgment is viewed as a personal attribute, it is necessary for effective problem solving / critical thinking, and its development needs to be incorporated in problem-solving/critical-thinking activities. With growth in problem-solving/critical-thinking skills, pupils also develop self-reliance and self-confidence, attributes that will assist them in solving real-world problems. Other attributes that contribute to problem-solving/critical-thinking skills include propensity for being well informed, willingness to consider various viewpoints, and fair-mindedness. Some of these attributes can be incorporated in problem-solving/critical-thinking activities, and some are considered outcomes of emotional-type learning to be examined later.

- ❐ Indeed, the importance of developing critical thinking skills and related personal attributes is underscored in the literature on teaching. In the literature, we read expressions like the following:
- ❐ "Not the learning of texts, but the solving of problems is the desideratum."
- ❐ "Honest thinking is the goal."
- ❐ "One of the chief aims of science teaching should be to train children to use the scientific method in the solution of problems."
- ❐ "The chief aim of education is to teach pupils to think, not to make their minds cold storage plants."
- ❐ "Unless we train our young people to think, democracy cannot endure."

It is clear that the field of education needs teachers who understand how to lead students to develop problem-solving/critical-thinking skills and who recognize the importance of personal attributes in the problem-solving/critical-thinking process.

Application Exercises

- ❐ A piece of ice is put into a glass, and then water is poured into the glass until the level of the water is even with the top of the glass. When the ice melts, will water run over the edge? Will the level of the water be lower? Or will the level remain the same? How much guessing will some children undertake in determining the answer? Is some scientific information needed to find the correct answer?

- ❐ Columbus had no facts to validate that the world is round, yet he was convinced that it was round. What led to his strong conviction?

- ❐ What should women and men be permitted to wear when they teach? Ask several children or adults this question and keep a record of the reasons given for the conclusions drawn. Are conclusions based on fact, opinion, prejudice, experience, or personal convenience?

- ❐ What is fallacy in reasoning? Give several illustrations.

- ❐ Research shows that some students in high school take "stiff" courses, such as foreign languages, mathematics, and science. These courses lend themselves to the development of better reasoning skills than do "soft" courses. If good thinkers are needed, children at the elementary grades also should be required to engage in curriculum that builds critical-thinking/reasoning skills so they will be prepared for the "stiff" courses in high school. What do you think?

- ❐ Teachers often say to children, "Think!" What do they usually mean by this? What is the best way to develop thinking ability in children?

- ❐ Today it appears that much emphasis in reading programs at the elementary school level is placed upon criteria-referenced testing, with the greatest emphasis upon word-analysis skills. Why is the emphasis shifting to word-analysis skills? What has brought about this shift? What effect will this shift have on children's learning if greater emphasis is not placed on problem-solving skills?

❒ Despite the teachers' efforts, some children will think deeper and faster than their classmates. Enumerate a number of factors responsible for the difference in ability to think.

❒ Regardless of how conscientiously a teacher works at teaching, a teacher never teaches a child anything but instead helps the child learn. Explain why this is true.

PART 4

PROBLEM-SOLVING-TYPE LEARNING: IN LIGHT OF RECENT RESEARCH

Introduction

In reviewing the literature, one finds that a significant amount of research has been conducted in the area of problem solving / critical thinking. Carline underscored the necessity for leading youngsters to develop problem-solving/critical-thinking skills and related personal attributes or dispositions. The necessity for including critical-thinking skills as outcomes of student learning in today's schools is equally clear in current literature. Teachers need to address the results of recent research as they design instruction and plan activities for today's classrooms.

Definition

In general, the term *critical thinking* refers to the higher-order thinking skills and requires individuals to engage in complex processes. Ennis (1985) pointed out that critical thinking is often linked with the upper levels of Bloom's Taxonomy, especially with the upper three levels: analysis, synthesis, and evaluation. Ennis (1985), however, contended that Bloom's Taxonomy is too vague and lacks criteria for evaluation of outcomes to guide curriculum development, teaching, and assessment for critical thinking. Ennis (1985) provided a working definition of critical thinking: "Critical thinking is reasonable reflective thinking that is focused on deciding what to believe or do" (46). He contended that critical thinking in this sense consists of integrated dispositions and abilities. Examples of some dispositions include being open-minded, paying attention to the whole situation, finding reasons, and attempting to stay well informed. Examples of some key abilities/skills include identifying and focusing on a question, observing and judging reports, making deductions and inductions, inferring explanations, and evaluating and judging interpretations.

In terms of critical thinking, Halpern (1998) noted:

> Critical thinking is purposeful, reasoned, and goal-directed. It is the kind of thinking involved in solving problems, formulating inferences, calculating likelihoods, and making decisions. Critical thinkers use these skills appropriately,

without prompting, and usually with conscious intent in a variety of settings. (450–451)

Halpern (1998) further noted:

> Critical thinking skills are often referred to as higher order cognitive skills to differentiate them from simpler (i.e., lower order) thinking skills. Higher order skills are relatively complex; require judgment, analysis, and synthesis; and are not applied in a rote or mechanical manner. Higher order thinking is thinking that is reflective, sensitive to the context, and self-monitored. (451)

According to Angelo (1995), "Most formal definitions characterize critical thinking as the intentional application of rational higher order thinking skills, such as analysis, synthesis, inference, and evaluation" (5). Beyer (1995) offered a simple definition: "Critical thinking ... means making reasoned judgments" (8). Thus, according to Beyer, critical thinking is a disciplined way of thinking that one uses for assessing the validity of something seen, read, and/or heard. Lai (2011) shared that educators are now quite aware of the importance of critical-thinking skills as outcomes of student learning. She also contended, "Critical thinking includes ... analyzing arguments, making inferences, using inductive or deductive reasoning, judging or evaluating, and making decisions or solving problems" (2).

It is apparent that Carline's definition of problem solving / critical thinking is similar to current definitions. His emphasis on inductive and deductive reasoning reflects much of what is involved in the reasoning process as described today.

Focus on Background Knowledge and Intelligence

As expressed in the literature, critical thinking requires both knowledge of the subject matter and effective application of essential critical-thinking skills. Kompf and Bond (2001) indicated that critical thinking includes knowledge and intelligence in addition to problem solving, decision making, metacognition, rational thinking, and reasoning skills. According to Mayer and Wittrock (2006), different kinds of knowledge, including facts, concepts, strategies, procedures, and beliefs about one's problem-solving skills, are required for successful problem solving. They contended that problem solving refers to "cognitive processing directed at achieving a goal when no solution method is obvious to the problem solver" (287). They noted that problem solving occurs within the problem solver's cognitive system and is inferred from a person's behavior. They indicated also that problem solving is a process that involves applying cognitive processes and relies on the knowledge and skill of the problem solver, and they provided examples of problem-solving occurrence, such as students effectively addressing the causes of a major war, explaining how the respiratory or other systems work after reading a relevant textbook, and/or reaching a solution for a complex mathematics word problem.

Willingham (2007) indicated that educators generally support the notion that a goal of education in our classrooms is to enable students to think critically, which requires knowledge of the content/issues. Basically, as he defined it, critical thinking consists of seeing both sides of an issue, being open to new evidence that refutes one's ideas, applying reasoning in an impartial manner, demanding evidence for claims, making deductions and inferring conclusions from the facts available, and solving problems.

Further, Willingham (2007) said that there are specific types of critical thinking that are characteristic of different subject matter, so we often refer to "thinking like a scientist" or "thinking like a historian." He questioned, however, whether critical thinking actually can be taught and went on to say that the processes of thinking are intertwined with the content of domain knowledge. He contended that if students are asked to look at an issue from various perspectives, they may not be able to do so if they know little about the issue. He focused on the nature of critical thinking, explained why it is so difficult to think critically and to teach others to do so, and examined how students become skillful in applying a specific type of critical thinking; namely, thinking scientifically. He contended that critical thinking is not a set of skills that can be implemented at will in any context. Essentially, he stressed that critical thinking is very much dependent on domain knowledge and practice. Thus, he underscored the need for sufficient background knowledge for critical thinking and stressed the importance of student practice. Further, he framed critical thinking as having three key features. His response to how cognitive scientists define critical thinking is as follows:

> From the cognitive scientists' point of view, the mental activities that are typically called critical thinking are actually a subset of three types of thinking: reasoning, making judgments and decisions, and problem solving. I say that critical thinking is a subset of these because we think in these ways all the time, but only sometimes in a critical way. Deciding to read this article, for example, is not critical thinking. But carefully weighing the evidence it presents in order to decide whether or not to believe what it says is. Critical reasoning, decision making, and problem solving, which, for brevity's sake, I will refer to as critical thinking—have three key features: effectiveness, novelty, and self-direction. Critical thinking is effective in that it avoids common pitfalls, such as seeing only one side of an issue, discounting new evidence that disconfirms your ideas, reasoning from passion rather than logic, failing to support statements with evidence, and so on. Critical thinking is novel in that you don't simply remember a solution or a situation that is similar enough to guide you. For example, solving a complex but familiar physics problem by applying a multi-step algorithm isn't critical thinking because you are really drawing on memory to solve the problem. But devising a new algorithm is critical thinking. Critical thinking is self-directed in that the thinker must be calling the shots: we wouldn't give a student much credit for critical thinking if the teacher were prompting each step he took. (11)

Carline clearly emphasized the need for students to have knowledge of facts or a knowledge base before they can be expected to appropriately apply reasoning and related skills and attributes. He stressed the need to provide students the opportunity to gain the necessary knowledge and facts prior to assigning problem-solving/critical-thinking tasks, and he acknowledged the clear distinction between critical thinking and rote memorization of facts.

Dispositions Involved in Critical Thinking

In addition to critical-thinking processes, related abilities, and background knowledge, it is generally understood that critical thinking involves "dispositions," or habits, as Ennis (1985) noted when defining critical thinking. Such dispositions are distinct from skills and background knowledge. In 1990, the American Philosophical Association sponsored a cross-disciplinary panel to complete a two-year Delphi project, resulting in a conceptualization of critical thinking that included two dimensions: cognitive skills and affective dispositions. The ideal critical thinker demonstrates dispositions referred to as attitudes, or habits of mind, including open- and fair-mindedness, curiosity regarding a wide range of issues, desire to become and remain well- informed, respect for and willingness to reconsider viewpoints, and willingness to consider different points of view. Lai (2011) indicated that background knowledge is a necessary but insufficient requirement for enabling critical thinking in a given subject area. According to Lai, critical thinking involves dispositions, in addition to sufficient background knowledge and cognitive skills. She noted, "These dispositions, which can be viewed as attitudes or habits of mind, include open-and fair-mindedness, inquisitiveness, flexibility, a propensity or inclination to seek reason, a desire to be well informed, and a respect for and willingness to entertain diverse viewpoints" (2).

In a study involving a group of gifted and talented fourth-graders, Connerly (2006) focused on a combination of affective and cognitive skills and on the intellectual standards of clarity, accuracy, relevance, logic, and fair-mindedness as applied to students' thinking. The materials and approach used were taken from *The Miniature Guide to Critical Thinking for Children* (Elder 2001) and the teacher's manual for this material (Elder 2002). Pre- and postsurveys demonstrated increased understanding and personal application of the standards.

Beyer (1995) examined key elements or aspects of critical thinking and noted the importance of dispositions that include remaining skeptical and open-minded, such as respecting evidence and reasoning, observing different points of view, and demonstrating willingness to accept other viewpoints when reason warrants. Critical thinking also involves ability to apply criteria or conditions that must be met for judging something as authentic and credible. Criteria used include standards for judging something credible as a statement that is based on trustworthy sources and accurate facts. Also, critical thinking involves ability to identify, assess, and create arguments that are precise, clearly reasoned, and based on believable evidence; infer a conclusion from one/more premises; view claims and statements from different perspectives;

and use strategies such as questioning and making judgments. Developing an inquiring mind may well be a key to improved critical thinking (King 1995).

Carline stressed the need for developing dispositions/attitudes mentioned here. He focused on the importance of teaching children the dispositions/attitudes required for critical thinking and underscored their centrality to problem-solving activity, personal development, and navigation of everyday challenges requiring application of reasoning skills.

Common Core State Standards and Critical Thinking

When developing the Common Core State Standards (CCSS), educators focused on critical thinking as well. As reflected in the CCSS, critical thinking is a learning skill required for high school graduates. The CCSS include critical thinking as a cross-disciplinary skill that is necessary for college and workforce success. Since 2010, a number of states across the nation have adopted the CCSS at each K–12 grade level for English and mathematics. Teachers, parents, and experts in the field of education designed the standards to better prepare students for postsecondary success. As Kirst and Torlakson (2013) shared in the *California Common Core Standards: English Language Arts and Literacy in History / Social Studies, Science, and Technical Subjects*:

> The standards establish what it means to be a literate person in the twenty-first century. Students learn to closely read and analyze works of literature and an array of nonfiction text in an exploding print and digital world. They use research and technology to sift through a staggering amount of information available and engage in collaborative conversations, sharing and reforming viewpoints through a variety of written and speaking applications. The CA CCSS for ELA/Literacy help build creativity and innovation, critical thinking and problem solving, collaboration and communication. (v)

In addition to observing the CCSS for ELA/Literacy, English language arts teachers are encouraged to collaborate with their colleagues who teach academic content subjects so that responsibility for students' literacy skills is shared through an integrated literacy model across the curriculum.

In mathematics, as noted in *California Common Core State Standards: Mathematics (2013)*, there are standards for mathematical practice and standards for mathematical content at each grade level. The standards for mathematical practice, which are essentially the same at each grade level, address overarching habits of mind of successful mathematical thinkers. The standards include making sense of problems and persevering in solving them; reasoning abstractly and quantitatively; constructing viable arguments and critiquing reasoning of others; modeling with mathematics; using appropriate tools strategically; attending to precision; looking for and making use of structure; and looking for and expressing regularity in repeated reasoning (3).

Teachers are encouraged, in light of these standards, to design specific curricular and instructional strategies to use in the classroom. In addition, as the standards were developed, educators, parents, and experts addressed assessment of learning outcomes, as the goal was to improve education by implementing both standards and aligned assessments. Two state consortia, the Partnership for Assessment of Readiness for College and Careers and the Smarter Balanced Assessment Consortium, were formed to design assessments aligned with the new standards.

In 2013, the Smarter Balanced Governing States formed state leadership teams (SLTs) and state networks of educators (SNEs), involving almost two thousand educators to develop the Digital Library. The Digital Library is an outstanding online collection of instructional and professional learning resources contributed by educators and aligned with the CCSS. Many of these resources focus on guiding students through the critical-thinking process in various disciplines as teachers implement formative assessment when leading students to reach the standards. The Smarter Balanced Assessment Consortium's goal is to ensure that all students leave high school prepared for postsecondary success. For resources to be accepted for posting in the Digital Library, they must incorporate one or more attributes of formative assessment. As well, Carline stressed the need to implement formative assessment as students progress through problem-solving/reasoning activities assigned.

Further, in terms of standards, the National Council of Teachers of Mathematics (NCTM) identified problem solving as central to the standards for mathematics that they updated in 2000, and since that time, conceptual understanding and reasoning have received much focus. Maccini and Gagnon

(2002) reported on the NCTM standards and indicated, "Standards address problem-solving and reasoning skills deemed essential for an increasingly technological society and future employment" (326). They noted that a key focus of the NCTM standards is on "conceptual understanding and reasoning rather than rule-driven memorization" (326).

Need for Direct Instruction

Thinking-skills research clearly supports direct instruction of critical thinking. Nisbett, Fong, Lehman, and Cheng (1987) reported that even brief formal training in making inferences may improve one's use of reasoning about events in everyday life. In fact, Lehman, Lempert, and Nisbett (1988) proposed a version of a formal discipline of reasoning, in light of the literature that describes the positive effects of training in the foundations of reasoning.

Halpern (1998) indicated that evidence reveals that critical thinking can be learned when appropriate instruction is provided, and it does transfer to different knowledge domains. She noted, "Fortunately, there already are powerful models of human learning that can be used as a guide for the redesign of education for thinking" (451).

Cotton (1991) summarized findings from the thinking-skills research reviewed for the 1991 report supporting the need to teach thinking skills in our schools. Reasons cited for providing students thinking-skills instruction include a necessity of thinking skills in our rapidly changing, technologically oriented world; a great need for well-developed thinking skills, as demonstrated by students in general; and research results demonstrating that creative and critical thinking abilities can be taught and learned.

Cotton (1991) incorporated in the summary of the report a number of points about critical-thinking/thinking skills, noting that instruction in thinking skills promotes intellectual growth and gains in academic achievement and that research supports instruction in various specific creative and critical-thinking skills, study techniques, and metacognitive skills. She indicated that the instructional approaches found to be effective include redirection, probing and reinforcement, asking higher-order questions during discussions with students, and lengthening wait-time for student response. In addition, she shared that computer-assisted instruction is effective in improving students' thinking skills and their intellectual growth and achievement and that several commercially prepared thinking-skills instructional programs have been found to be effective.

As Cotton (1991) noted in the report, while training teachers to teach thinking skills is warranted, effective thinking-skills instruction relies on many factors, including administrative support and selection of the best instructional approaches for given groups of students. She reported that both infused thinking-skills instruction and separate curricula in critical thinking can lead to increased student performance, and elements of both are often combined for best results. Cotton (1991) noted that overall, student performance has improved as a result of direct teaching and inferential learning of thinking skills, and a positive, stimulating, encouraging classroom environment and administrative support are needed for effective thinking-skills instruction (9–10). Since Cotton's review, much research has been conducted that supports thinking-skills instruction.

Oliver and Utermohlen (1995) stressed the need for instruction in critical thinking in our schools. as students need to "develop and effectively apply critical thinking skills to their academic studies, to the complex problems they will find, and to the critical choices they will be forced to make as a result of the information explosion and other rapid technological changes" (1).

Abrami et al. (2008) analyzed 117 studies to determine the impact of instruction on the development and enhancement of critical-thinking skills and dispositions. They reported that empirical evidence has demonstrated that in order to increase problem-solving/critical-thinking (CT) skills, educators must make critical-thinking objectives explicit in courses, and that critical thinking needs to be included in teacher-preparation programs and in ongoing professional development. Abrami et al. (2008) indicated:

> Making CT requirements a clear and important part of course design is associated with larger instructional effects. Developing CT skills separately and then applying them to course content explicitly works best; immersing students in thought-provoking subject matter without explicit use of CT principles was least effective. (1121)

Dewar (2009) supported critical-thinking instruction and noted that while students become better learners when they must explain how they solve the problems confronting them, studies show that students become much better problem solvers when they are taught explicit critical-thinking skills. Dewar (2009) noted that such skills include analyzing analogies, identifying relevant information, constructing and recognizing valid deductive arguments, testing hypotheses, and recognizing common reasoning fallacies, among others.

Zohar, Weinberger, and Tamir (1994) tested 678 seventh-grade students on analytical skills and then randomly assigned some students to receive critical-thinking lessons as part of the biology curriculum. Students in the experimental group were taught to recognize logical fallacies, analyze arguments, test hypotheses, and distinguish between evidence and interpretation of evidence. Students in the control group received instruction from the same textbook in biology but did not receive critical-thinking instruction. At the end of the study, students were retested. The experimental group students demonstrated greater improvement in analytical skills, not just for biology but for solving everyday problems.

In a critical-thinking initiative conducted with the West Side High School, Crook (2006) reported that the goal for all students was to increase their use of critical thinking through reading and writing activities in response to higher-order questions. In the report's summary, it is stated that students' critical thinking increased in all areas of the curriculum, and the students became better critical thinkers. As a result of critical-thinking instruction, developed by the Foundation for Critical Thinking, students' SAT and ACT test scores significantly increased. In fact, results on the ACT were the highest in school history, and on the SAT, the various scores were either the highest or second or third highest in the school's history. The Foundation for Critical Thinking is a nonprofit organization that is committed to fostering critical thinking worldwide, and it promotes change in education and society through the development of improved critical thinking.

Instructional Strategies: Schema-Based Problem-Solving Strategies

With regard to teaching mathematical skills, researchers have conducted numerous studies in the area of schema-based problem-solving strategies and other instructional strategy areas. According to Na (2009), "a schema is a chunk of information stored in long-term memory, specifying how a number of concepts are related to one another" (26). Chen (1999) noted that the term *schema* is defined as a basic description of a number of problems with a common structure that require a similar manner of solution.

In mathematics, schema-based problem-solving strategies for classroom implementation are described in the literature, particularly for solving word problems. Powell (2011) indicated, "A schema is a framework for solving a problem. With a schema, students are taught to recognize problems as falling within word-problem types and to apply a problem solution method that matches the problem type" (94). Powell (2011) noted:

> Word-problem instruction using schemas differs from typical word-problem instruction (e.g., key words, checklist of steps) because students first identify a word problem as belonging to a problem *type* and then use a specific problem-type *schema* to solve the problem. In conventional word-problem instruction, students may organize word-problem information or follow a mnemonic device to work step-by-step through the problem; however, students are not taught to determine a problem type and solve word problems according to a problem-type of schema. (97)

Powell (2011) referred to two schema approaches, called *schema-based instruction*, which teaches students to use schematic diagrams; and *schema-broadening instruction*, which is "similar to schema-based instruction in that students read the word problem and select a schema(from thee taught schemas) to solve the word problems. Schema-broadening instruction differs from schema-based instruction because students are taught to transfer their knowledge of problem types to recognize problems with novel features ... as belonging to a problem type for which they know a solution" (100).

Powell concluded that whether schema-based or schema-broadening instruction is used, research conducted "demonstrates that students at risk for or with LD may benefit from explicit word-problem instruction that incorporates schemas" (108).

Na (2009) noted that schema-based instruction leads students to approach a mathematics problem by asking them to focus on the underlying semantic or problem structure and that doing so facilitates conceptual understanding and application of skills. In a study focused on providing sixth- and seventh-grade middle school students with learning disabilities schema-based intervention on mathematical word problem-solving skills for one-step multiplication and division word problems, Na (2009) reported that schema-based intervention helped the students acquire mathematical word problem-solving skills, in that their performance substantially improved after they received instruction.

In this study the specific problem-solving procedural stages included identifying the pattern or relationship present in each word problem; creating a mental model of the problem; determining a way the schema can be used to plan and set up a math equation; and carrying out the steps of the plan or using techniques that facilitate problem solution. The instructional materials and word problem types used were adapted from two programs of schema-based intervention that Jitendra (2007) had developed with her colleagues, including scripted lessons for each phase of instruction, note sheets for students, checklists, and diagrams (as cited in Na 2009).

In terms of transferring the schema-based strategy to solving real-world problems, Na (2009) noted that each student's accuracy performance on the generalization tests improved, exceeding the criterion level. Further, students maintained test scores across the postintervention phase and evaluated the strategy as enjoyable and useful.

Fuchs et al. (2008) conducted a study that showed the benefit of schema-based tutoring intervention or schema-broadening instruction, as described by Powell (2011), in teaching third-grade students to solve word problems. They noted, "In contrast to Jitendra et al., however, we incorporate an additional instructional component by explicitly teaching students to transfer their problem-solving skills" (Fuchs et al. 2008, 159). They indicated that they taught students to "transfer their problem solving skills to problems that include irrelevant information, two-digit operands, missing information in the first or second positions in the algebraic equation, or relevant information in charts, graphs, or pictures" (167).

Fuchs et al. (2008) noted that the schema-based tutoring protocol that relied on the schema-broadening instruction taught students to do the following:

- Understand the underlying mathematical structure of the problem type.
- Recognize the basic schema for a problem type.
- Solve the problem type.
- Transfer so they recognize problems with novel superficial features as belonging to the problem type, or schema for which they know a problem solution. (161)

Results of this study revealed statistically significant effects for students receiving the schema-broadening tutoring. These findings demonstrated the effectiveness of the schema-broadening tutoring protocol for preventing word-problem deficits for third-grade students who have math and reading deficits (Fuchs et al. 2008).

Researchers have noted that solving various apparently different but structurally similar problems facilitates development of generalized problem-solving skills and schema knowledge (Chen 1999) and provides students with opportunity for practice. The shift is in providing such experience to students.

Other Instructional Strategies/Techniques

Much research supports not only direct instruction in critical-thinking skills but instruction that focuses on transfer of these skills across various knowledge domains, as well as instruction that incorporates other strategies designed to facilitate critical thinking. Halpern (1998) noted, "It is clear that successful pedagogy that can serve as a basis for the enhancement of thinking will have to incorporate ideas about the way in which learners organize knowledge and internally represent it and the way these representations change and resist change when new information is encountered" (451). She further noted:

> The model that I am proposing for teaching thinking skills so they will transfer across domains of knowledge consists of four parts: (a) dispositional or attitudinal component, (b) instruction and practice with critical-thinking skills, (c) structure-training activities designed to facilitate transfer across contexts, and (d) a metacognitive component used to direct and assess thinking. Each of these components is grounded in theories and research in cognitive psychology. (451)

Halpern proposed a taxonomy of critical thinking skills to include verbal reasoning skills; argument analysis skills; skills in thinking as hypothesis testing; likelihood and uncertainty; and decision-making and problem-solving skills (452). She also stressed the need to teach critical-thinking skills so that they can be transferred, to use instructional tasks that mandate thoughtful analysis and synthesis, to use many kinds of examples of relevant tasks and questions, and to incorporate metacognitive monitoring features during instruction. Lai (2011) also urged instructors to provide explicit instruction in critical thinking and to teach students to transfer skills to new contexts.

Mayer and Wittrock (2006) suggested that, in addition to promoting problem-solving transfer or the ability to apply what was learned in different situations/content, some methods/strategies intended to promote meaningful learning should include providing advance organizers that "prime" relevant prior knowledge when learning and asking learners to orally articulate a text or part of a text they are reading. In addition to advance organizers, other strategies they recommended for promoting meaningful learning include providing "worked out examples," along with comments on the solutions and providing some kind of guidance to students as they work to solve problems.

Wittrock (1974) described meaningful learning as a generative process, when learners try to make sense of the information presented and engage in active cognitive processing during learning as they generate their own cognitive meanings. In this process, learners integrate new ideas into memory and link new concepts with ideas already in their long-term memory. Generative learning focuses on learners being active participants in the instructional process as they construct knowledge using new information and integrate it with prior knowledge and experience. Fiorella and Mayer (2015) noted three cognitive processes involved (1) selecting information to attend to (selecting); (2) mentally organizing incoming information into a coherent cognitive structure in working memory (organizing); and (3) integrating pieces of information with prior knowledge activated from long-term memory (integrating). They cited eight generative evidence-based learning strategies that improve learning as follows: summarizing, mapping, drawing, imagining, self-testing, self-explaining, teaching, and enacting.

Anderman (2010) indicated:

> In 1974, Wittrock presented his generative model of learning to the research community. Wittrock's model effectively integrated several important processes and emphasized the important roles of (a) cognition, (b) prior knowledge, (c) transfer, and (d) generation of human learning. (55)

According to Anderman, reciprocal teaching strategies encourage generation of new ideas that can enhance self-efficacy and learning, and he noted:

> In reciprocal teaching, students are taught four basic reading strategies: summarizing, asking questions, clarifying, and predicting. These strategies generally are taught in a social setting, with a teacher or more experienced individual providing scaffolded instruction in the strategies. Three of these strategies (summarizing, asking questions, and predicting) are generative in nature. (58)

In terms of instructional strategies, Lai shared the following:

> Cooperative or collaborative learning methods hold promise as a way of stimulating cognitive development, along with constructivist approaches that place students at the center of the learning process. Teachers should model critical thinking in their instruction and provide concrete examples for illustrating abstract concepts that students will find salient. (43)

She further noted:

> Educators are urged to use open-ended problem types and to consider learning activities and assessment tasks that make use of authentic, real-world problem contexts. In addition, critical thinking assessments should use ill-structured problems that require students to go beyond recalling or restating learned information and also require students to manipulate the information in new or novel contexts. (44)

Lai indicated that the ill-structured problems should have more than one solution that can be defended, and the materials used should "embed contradictions" that will activate critical thinking. She further noted that the assessment tasks should be designed to require students to provide evidence in support of judgments or claims made (44).

Others also focused on processes found in the real world and on connecting students' knowledge and experiences with new learning. Fennimore and Tinzmann (1990) stressed the need to promote in-depth learning; integrate content and process by teaching students content through processes met in the real world, including decision making, problem solving, and evaluating; teaching processes holistically versus using the isolated skills approach; leading students to develop a deep understanding of important concepts and processes for dealing with those concepts and authentic tasks; and sequencing tasks to facilitate holistic performance of complex tasks in increasingly challenging environments as students build self-confidence. They also noted the importance of considering and expanding upon the experiences and knowledge that students bring with them by connecting those experiences and knowledge to new learning. Further, they emphasized promoting problem solving and higher-order thinking skills as part of the curriculum, rather than treating them in isolation (Fennimore and Tinzmann 1990).

Additional strategies for teaching problem solving / critical thinking include classroom assessment techniques (Angelo 1995); case study / discussion method (McDade 1995); and conference-style learning, where the teacher facilitates learning as students read assigned material, form analytic questions, identify challenging issues, and demonstrate respect for the viewpoints of others during group dialogue (Underwood and Wald 1995).

King (1995) discussed the inquiry-based approach, where students are taught a model of inquiry and how to apply it in cooperative learning contexts in the classroom and in individual study environments. This approach involves teaching students to develop a habit of inquiry by asking thoughtful questions of themselves and others about lecture and textbook material and about class discussions. King noted, "I believe that the hallmark of a critical thinker is an inquiring mind. Simply put, good thinkers are good questioners" (13). King suggested that to teach students how to ask thoughtful questions, teachers should give students the structure and guidance of exemplar questions. Questions such as "What does this mean?" "What is the nature of …?" and "What is the evidence for this?" reflect the kind of questions that students should ask. According to King, "Asking questions such as these and using them to understand the world around us is what characterizes critical thinking" (13).

Carline as well stressed the need to ask the right kinds of questions in order to provide students the opportunity for problem solving. He also emphasized the need to provide students adequate practice and the opportunity to eventually solve problems independently. He mentioned, however, that in order for teachers to arrange appropriate problem-solving activities, they must understand the child's capacity to think, and they need to focus on materials of interest to students when engaging them in reading and problem-solving activities. As he noted, children must learn to read printed material and to learn from it, so educators must find a way to instill a love of reading and learning. With self-confidence and love of reading and learning, children will be better enabled to learn and apply appropriate problem-solving/critical-thinking/reasoning skills.

It can be concluded that when teaching critical thinking in the classroom, teachers should use good models of instruction that support student engagement in higher-order thinking skills; provide numerous opportunities for practice; model the use of strategies using appropriate materials and technology that help maximize learning; use whole class, cooperative, small group, and independent learning strategies in order to facilitate critical thinking; and instill a love of reading and learning. Implementing these practices will serve our students well.

References for Part 4—Problem-Solving-Type Learning

Abrami, P. C., R. M. Bernard, E. Borokhovski, A. Wade, M. A. Surkes, R. Tamin, and P. A. Zhang. 2008. "Instructional Interventions Affecting Critical Thinking Skills and Dispositions: A Stage 1 Meta-analysis." *Review of Educational Research* 78, no. 4: 1102–1134.

American Philosophical Association. 1990. "Critical Thinking: A Statement of Expert Consensus for Purposes of Educational Assessment and Instruction. The Delphi Report: Research Findings and Recommendations Prepared for the Committee on Pre-college Philosophy." P. Facione (Project Director). ERIC Doc. No: ED 315–423.

Anderman, E. M. 2010. "Reflections on Wittrock's Generative Model of Learning: A Motivation Perspective." *Educational Psychologist* 45, no. 1: 55–60.

Angelo, T. A. 1995. "Beginning the Dialogue: Thoughts on Promoting Critical Thinking: Classroom Assessment for Critical Thinking." *Teaching of Psychology* 22, no. 1: 6–7.

Beyer, B. K. 1995. *Critical Thinking.* Bloomington, IN: Phi Delta Kappa Educational Foundation.

California Common Core State Standards: Mathematics. 2013. Sacramento, CA: California Department of Education.

Chen, Z. 1999. "Schema Induction in Children's Analogical Problem Solving." *Journal of Educational Psychology* 91, no. 4: 703–715.

Connerly, D. 2006. "Teaching Critical Thinking Skills to Fourth Grade Students Identified as Gifted and Talented." Submitted in partial fulfillment for master's of education in collaborative teaching and learning, Graceland University, Cedar Rapids, Iowa, December 2006. www.criticalthinking.org/page/title/685.

Cotton, K. 1991. "Close-Up #11: Teaching Thinking Skills." (November) Retrieved from Northwest Regional Educational Laboratory's School

Improvement Research Series. www.nwrel.orghttp://educationnorthwest.org/6/cu11.html.

Crook, D. 2006. "Substantive Critical Thinking as Developed by the Foundation for Critical Thinking Proves Effective in Raising SAT and ACT Test Scores at West Side High School." *NCA Final Documentation Report January, 2006.* www.criticalthinking.org/pages/substantive-critical-thinking-as-developed-by-the-foundation-for-critical-thinking-proves-effective-in-raising-SAT-and-ACT-test-scores/632.

Dewar, G. 2009. "Teaching Critical Thinking: An Evidence-Based Guide, 2009–2012." www.parentingscience.com/teaching-critical-thinking.html.

Dewey, J. 1910. *How We Think.* New York, NY: D.C. Heath & Co. Publishers.

Elder, L. 2001. *The Miniature Guide to Critical Thinking for Children.* Dillon Beach, CA: Foundation for Critical Thinking.

Elder, L. 2002. *Teacher's Manual: The Miniature Guide to Critical Thinking for Children.* Dillon Beach, CA: Foundation for Critical Thinking.

Ennis, R. H. 1985. "A Logical Basis for Measuring Critical Thinking Skills." *Educational Leadership* 43, no. 2: 44–48. www.ascd.org/ASCD/pdfjournals/ed_lead/el_198510_ennis.pdf.

Fennimore, T. F., and M. B. Tinzmann. 1990. *What Is Thinking Curriculum?* Oak Brook, IL: North Central Regional Education Laboratory. www.asa3.org/ASA/education/think/thinking-ft.pdf.

Fiorella, L., and E. Mayer. 2015. *Learning as a Generative Activity: Eight Learning Strategies That Promote Understanding.* New York, NY: Cambridge University Press.

Fuchs, L. S., P. M. Seethaler, S. R. Powell, D. Fuchs, C. L. Hamlett, and J. M. Fletcher. 2008. "Effects of Preventative Tutoring on the Mathematical Problem Solving of Third-Grade Students with Math and Reading

Difficulties." *Exceptional Children* 74, no. 2: 155–173. www.ncbi.nim.nih.gov/pmc/articlesPMCID: PMC2832201.

Halpern, D. F. 1998. "Teaching Critical Thinking for Transfer across Domains: Disposition, Skills, Structure Training, and Metacognitive Monitoring." *American Psychologist* 53, no. 4: 449–455.

Jitendra, A. K. 2007. *Solving Math Word Problems: Teaching Students with Learning Disabilities Using Schema-Based Instruction.* Austin, TX: Pro-Ed.

Kelley, E. C. 1969. *Humanizing the Education of Children.* Washington, DC: National Education Association, an Elementary Kindergarten Nursery Education (EKNE) Publication.

King, A. 1995. "Designing the Instructional Process to Enhance Critical Thinking across the Curriculum: Inquiring Minds Really Do Want to Know: Using Questioning to Teach Critical Thinking." *Teaching of Psychology* 22, no. 1: 13–17.

Kirst, M. W., and T. Torlakson. 2013. "A Message from the State Board of Education and the State Superintendent of Public Instruction." In *California Common Core State Standards: English Language Arts and Literacy in History / Social Studies, Science, and Technical Subjects* (March). Sacramento, CA: California Department of Education.

Kompf, M., and R. Bond. 2001. "Critical Reflection in Adult Education." In *The Craft of Teaching Adults*, edited by T. Barer-Stein and M. Kompf, 21–38. Toronto, ON: Irwin Publishing.

Lai, E. R. 2011. *Critical Thinking: A Literature Review (Research Report).* New York, NY: Pearson. www.pearsonassessments.com/research.

Lehman, D. R., R. O. Lempert, and R. E. Nisbett. 1988. "The Effects of Graduate Training on Reasoning: Formal Discipline and Thinking about Everyday-Life Events." *American Psychologist* 43: 431–442.

Maccini, P., and J. C. Gagnon. 2002. "Perceptions and Applications of NCTM Standards by Special and General Education Teachers." *Exceptional Children* 68: 325–344.

Mayer, R. E., and M. C. Wittrock. 2006. "Problem Solving." In *Handbook of Educational Psychology*, edited by P. A. Alexander and P. H. Winne, 287-303. Mahwah, NJ: Lawrence Erlbaum Associates, Inc.

Mayer, R. E., and M. C. Wittrock. 2009. "Problem Solving." www.education.com/reference/article/problem-solving1.

McDade, S. A. 1995. "Case Study Pedagogy to Advance Critical Thinking." *Teaching of Psychology* 22, no. 1: 9–10.

Na, K. 2009. "The Effects of Schema-Based Intervention on the Mathematical Word Problem Solving Skills in Middle School Students with Learning Disabilities." UT Electronic Theses and Dissertations, Austin, TX: University of Texas Digital Repository.

National Council of Teachers of Mathematics. 2000. *Principles and Standards for School Mathematics*. Reston, VA: Author.

Nisbett, R. E., G. T. Fong, D. R. Lehman, and P. W. Cheng. 1987. "Teaching Reasoning." *Science* 238, no. 4827: 625–631.

Oliver, H., and R. Utermohlen (1995). "An Innovative Teaching Strategy: Using Critical Thinking to Give Students a Guide to the Future." ERIC Doc. No. ED 389 702.

Powell, S. R. 2011. "Solving Word Problems Using Schemas: A Review of the Literature." *Learning Disabilities Research and Practice* 26, no. 2: 94–108. 10.1111/j.1540-5826.2011.00329.x.

Underwood, M. K., and R. L. Wald. 1995. "Conference-Style Learning: A Method for Fostering Critical Thinking with Heart." *Teaching of Psychology* 22, no. 1: 24–28.

Willingham, D. T. 2007. "Critical Thinking: Why Is It So Hard to Teach?" *American Educator* (Summer): 8–19.

Wittrock, M. C. 1974. "Learning as a Generative Process." *Educational Psychologist* 11: 87–95.

Zohar, A., Y. Weinberger, and P. Tamir. 1994. "The Effect of the Biology Critical Thinking Project on the Development of Critical Thinking." *Journal of Research in Science Teaching* 31, no. 2: 183–196.

PART 5

EMOTIONAL-TYPE LEARNING: TIMELESS WISDOM

Introduction

Alan had just completed his junior year in high school. His grades were excellent, and as a token of work satisfactorily completed, his parents permitted him to work in a large supermarket. He hadn't worked there very long when he was called into the manager's office, where the manager said, "I'm very sorry to tell you that we must let you go. We've tried to tell you on several occasions how to work more efficiently, how to work with others here, and how to treat our customers. While working as a produce boy, as a food stocker, and as a sacker, you did not heed our suggestions. While you tried to get your work done, you rushed through it and did not make efficient use of time. As a result, you did not complete tasks neatly. When you continued to come in late and leave early, others here had to fill in for you and leave their own work unfinished. On a few occasions, after we spoke to you about how to work with your boss, you argued with him at length about how to stock shelves. Your habit of making disrespectful remarks to our customers turned some of them away. A few of them never returned to our store. I'm sorry that we must let you go, but we must safeguard our business interests."

When Alan returned home that day, he felt depressed and anxious. He stopped by my house next door to discuss what he had been told. I tried my best to share my perspectives with him regarding how to prevent recurrence.

For a person who had been given an opportunity to work at age 17 because he had succeeded academically in high school, what was responsible for his behavior? More specifically, what did Alan lack that hindered his effectiveness as a worker in the supermarket? In his case, personal attributes such as tolerance, punctuality, neatness, loyalty, self-control, and politeness were underdeveloped or not developed at all. As a result, he acted in a certain manner. His lack of these attributes influenced his conduct in an undesirable way. In short, he did not conduct himself properly. His ability to sack groceries, stock shelves, and trim produce was insufficient for success in the workplace. Honesty, fair play, truthfulness, patriotism, broad-mindedness, kindness, and self-reliance are other personal attributes that facilitate success in the workplace. Alan needed to develop these attributes as well. Attributes like these influence one's conduct and play a significant part in life so the development of such attributes will always be essential to teaching and learning.

Another experience, related by a school superintendent I knew personally, follows:

> I remember well, as a fifth-grader, how the poem "The Night Has a Thousand Eyes" won its way into my list of treasured poems.
>
> > The Night has a thousand eyes,
> > And the Day but one;
> > Yet the light of the bright world dies
> > With the dying sun.
> > The mind has a thousand eyes,
> > And the heart but one;
> > Yet the light of the whole life dies
> > When love is done.
> > —Francis William Bourdillon (1852–1921)
>
> With the aid of the teacher, we were led to discover what the thousand eyes of the night were; what the dying sun meant in the daily run of things; what the thousand eyes of the mind and the one of the heart were. But what a feeling came when the last two lines were experienced and lived! In that same classroom was a little girl who received from me the deepest devotion of my childhood heart. It was she who made my attendance record almost perfect; it was she who made the schoolroom more pleasant and appealing. It was her absence that brought gloom and darkness and longing when the cold or the rain kept her from school. And my young mind began to realize what her loss would mean to me if she were no longer there. Surely, the light would go out, and darkness would come. Indeed,
>
> > The light of the whole life dies
> > When love is done.

This story has deep implications for the classroom. A significant change takes place in people when they add certain works to their treasured list of poems. The addition of something worth treasuring is of vital importance. This cannot happen, however, unless they feel deep worth, unless they appreciate, unless they enjoy. A person who appreciates differs from the person who does not appreciate. The former has changed personally or has acquired an attribute that the latter has not. For the purpose of clarity, these attributes will be called "appreciations." They are attributes that are vital to the learning process. Appreciation attributes are numerous, some of them being appreciations of poetry, literature, art, music, science, history, ecology, beauty, and human nature. These appreciations determine how one can and will enjoy leisure time, how one can and will select hobbies, how one can and will use physical and mental energies in moments of recreation or leisure, and how one can and will relate to others.

Behind these two illustrations lies a broad and deeply hidden background of meanings and implications exceedingly important in the work of any teacher. They need to be examined further.

Conduct Attributes—Learning to Live and How to Make a Living

There are implications relative to the aims of living and of learning to make a living. Not all the real aims of living can be included in the one aim of making a living. Learning to live and learning how to make a living are two parts of complete living. The latter is never complete by itself, yet it is often the one part that receives all of the attention. In Alan's case, we see that a lack of certain personal attributes was directly responsible for his inability to do well in a real-life workplace situation. As mentioned earlier, in addition to attributes including punctuality, tolerance, self-control, and politeness that facilitate workplace success, personal attributes such as honesty, fair play, truthfulness, patriotism, broad mindedness, kindness, and self-reliance influence a person's conduct and enable one to succeed in the workplace.

Some personal attributes may be referred to as attitudes or perspectives. For example, we may say that one who obtains and weighs evidence has a critical attitude. It is important to understand that whatever these attributes are called, they do influence one's conduct. The person who weighs evidence before reaching conclusions will act in one way; the person who jumps to conclusions will act in another. Since conduct plays such a significant part in life, we should always treat the development of attributes as vital to teaching and learning.

Appreciation Attributes—Learning to Live

In addition to conduct attributes, appreciation attributes are essential when learning to live. Those who appreciate the fine arts, beauty in general, history, and science will engage in enriching activities that will determine, in part, how they live and nurture personal relationships.

In recent years much emphasis has been placed upon the value of personal attributes that influence one's appreciation for the arts, literature, music, and learning how to live and that influence one's propensity for developing meaningful and enriching relationships and contributing to one's community. What shall it profit our nation to spend millions of dollars on the education of young children in teaching them how to read, for example, and then find that they never want to read? Why stress everlasting skills without considering the manner in which these skills will be applied for the good of the individual and society? Why give a child power through learning without paying attention to the building up of character from which this power emanates? Surely the development of good citizens—strong and upright and noble characters—is a vital obligation of education. Development of appreciation attributes should be fostered simultaneously with all other objectives of learning. No chain is stronger than its weakest link. The chain of learning should have no weak links. The chain should not be weakened by the links of emotional learning. Teachers need to be very concerned with the personal development of children and youth—everlastingly and untiringly concerned.

The Development of Attributes

A significant difference exists between the attainment of personal attributes and other learning objectives. A complete awareness of this difference will enable one to select the psychologically sound activities in emotional type of learning. An analysis of your own learning over the years will help you to experience this difference. We will start with the assumption that you have one personal attribute truly and thoroughly inculcated, the attribute of fair play. As you are walking along the street, you see a big, husky boy, deliberately and unmercifully beating up on a much smaller boy. The big boy kicks the smaller boy, takes him by the neck, and thrusts his head into the snow. He shoves snow down the smaller boy's collar, plugs his ears and eyes with snow, and then keeps holding him down into the snow. Do you see this occurrence and walk on undisturbed? You do not. You possess a keen sense of fair play, and your heart beats in sympathy for the small boy and in outrage for the bully. You call for help, shout out at the big boy, or intercede in a safe manner. You are affected. Somehow or somewhere, you learned to treasure fair play.

How you gained that personal attribute is very important. Beginning with your own experience and assuming that you have the personal attribute of fair play, you might trace its development. You learned to believe in and stand for fair play, just as you learned to spell, write, and read. Yes, you learned fair play, and different activities were involved in the process. The chart below will assist you in understanding the sequence of activities that were involved.

Sequence of Stages in Analysis

The idea of fair play dawned upon you. You heard about, read about, or saw it. You became conscious about it in your living. You thought about it. You recalled situations involving fair play; there really was such a thing in living with others.	You began to feel that fair play was right; your best friends played fair. You were sorry once when you did use dishonest means to win. You were angry when another won from you by foul means. You felt that you would be fair; you resolved to be.	You practiced fair play; fair play became a rule in your conduct with others and others with you. Each exercise of fair play strengthened your beliefs in this attribute. You felt its value more deeply.	You interfere when fair play is violated. You play fair yourself, and you want to see fair play in all human relationships.

Many have concluded, however, that the emotional type of learning is the most difficult to direct, vastly more difficult than the sensory experience, memory, motor, or problem-solving/critical-thinking types of learning. We can specify clearly what should be done to direct pupils to acquire specific motor skills or to understand the memorization process when teaching them how to apply word-analysis skills in reading. It is quite easy to determine if these skills have been sufficiently learned and if pupils can use them in their lives. But not so with personal attributes. The greatest weakness in teaching is found in this more human side of education. Why should this be true? There are several reasons:

- This type of learning is least understood.
- It is inherently difficult.
- Teachers too often persist in teaching for personal attributes just as they teach for the acquisition of skills, with a gathering of facts and information; namely, by the hammering-in process.

Of these three reasons, the third accounts for most of the weaknesses in teaching the development of attributes because it includes the other two indirectly.

Stages in Development of Attributes

When analyzing the sequence of activities and stages of attribute development, it is helpful to consider the four stages in reverse order when teaching. Start with the idea, emotions, and practice, and conclude with the acquired attribute when it functions in living. This sequence, from bottom to top, summarizes the growth of a personal attribute such as fair play.

Attribute acquired when it functions in living
Practice
Emotions
Idea

The teacher can best succeed in directing emotional learning by understanding these successive stages through which children pass in gaining genuine conduct or appreciation attributes and by providing opportunities for pupils to demonstrate attributes during each stage of development. The first stage of attribute formation involves the foundation or beginning stage, when an idea is gained. There must be a beginning point in all learning, and in emotional learning that beginning point is an idea. When the linking of the words in the poem with the little girl in the schoolroom occurred, an idea was formed or born. This linking was real, true to life, true to experience. It was concrete, and it joined the poem with a dear reality in life. The idea was there, tangible and worthwhile. No amount of talking or forcing or moralizing can make someone form an idea. Another person can suggest and facilitate, but that person cannot force another to form an idea. The idea that really counts comes from within, from actual experience or reconstructed experience.

Further, while ideas come to children from a number of different sources, the manner in which they are presented takes two general paths. In facilitating the formation of children's ideas, the teacher can employ the direct or the indirect approach. If the idea is presented directly—that is, taught by openly addressing the particular conduct or appreciation attribute—the teaching is called direct. On the other hand, if the opportunity to gain the idea is provided without openly mentioning or addressing the attribute, the teaching is indirect. The following anecdote will show how David obtained an idea that started the development of a desirable attribute in his character.

Teacher: Good morning, David. We missed you over the last few days, but we're glad you're back. Were you ill, David?

David: Yes, I was ill, Miss Green. I had a bad cold, and I coughed a lot. When we studied about diseases and how they spread, we learned that colds could be spread by germs coughed or sneezed into the air, and we learned that people without colds catch colds by being where other people sneeze. When I got this cold, I thought I might give it to somebody else if I came to school, so I told my mother it wasn't right for me to give others a cold by going to school. Mother said that I was very thoughtful and that I should stay home.

Teacher: You did the right thing, David. I will help you with the lessons that you missed.

David's lesson was acquired indirectly. It was his idea; it was discovered without the aid of another person. At this time, it is important to note not only the idea but also the essence of the idea. The idea was right from David's heart and soul, direct from his experience and life, connected, perhaps, with the thought of how he had caught colds in the past that had been caused by the negligence of others, linked with the conduct of persons who violated principles of human relationships. Indeed, it is such ideas as these that strike home and start children on the journey to develop indelible conduct and appreciation attributes. Sometimes these kinds of ideas come from indirect teaching and at other times by direct facilitation, but these ideas must come. The ideas must take hold, and to do so they need the background of children's experiences, feelings, insight, judgment, and sense of value. Abstract discussions of such ideas mean little or nothing. Such discussions are generally unheeded and seldom understood, but an idea from within carries weight and gripping significance.

At times, direct teaching of ideas is necessary and effective. For example, no good mother allows her child to be dishonest. From the very first, she tries by direct teaching to lead her child to value and to see the need for being honest. So in teaching, many ideas leading to attribute formations are taught directly.

With direct teaching of ideas leading to attributes, as well as with indirect teaching, it is essential to understand the importance of pupil involvement, including the pupil's concern for the idea discussed and its significance to the pupil. Too often, teachers preach, moralize, and eulogize in order to stamp in the ideas sanctioned by model adults. Children listen, but they do not enter actively into the situations described. In direct teaching, a teacher must remember to play the part of a stimulator of ideas, not a drill master of ideas. The teacher leads but cannot drive. The teacher can ask questions or set situations, but the actual acceptance of ideas comes from within the child. If the child cannot accept ideas or is not so inclined, no outside force can make the child do so.

The second stage of attribute formation involves some warmth and feeling, some grip or emotional arousal connected with the attribute. The source of this arousal is within the child. The source, in turn, comprises the child's experiences, sense of values, notions of right and wrong, personal relationships, and connection with the child's world of ideas and ideals. The arousal gains momentum only as the child connects with the desired attributes. The source, then, of a child's learning in emotional type of learning is always the child and the personal standards that the child holds. The child's evaluations are evaluations of self. Failure in the child's learning occurs when external means are employed to force the attribute onto a child without regard for the child's accepting spirit within.

How best, then, can a teacher drive this inner emotional reaction and accepting spirit? One guiding principle seems to hold: the emotional reaction must be within the child's range of responses and reactions. Emotional reactions cannot be expected to extend to the outermost limits. The range is determined by the child's maturity/developmental level, experience, and knowledge. One would not expect a child to do the same amount and kind of physical labor as a healthy and robust adult. Neither should one expect a child to react emotionally to the same degree/level of an adult.

Further, since the emotional reaction does not occur without a stimulus, the nature of the stimulus demands consideration. This stimulus is an idea associated with some personal experience. Examine again the nature of the stimuli in the appreciation of the poem and in David's conduct when he was ill. In both instances, an idea was the stimulus—the starting point. Notice further that the ideas were not merely ideas, factual and cold in nature. These ideas were warm and touching. They related to the experiences and lives of the two persons. They aroused the response driven by the emotions. The ideas and emotional response were combined.

The third stage of attribute formation involves providing opportunities for children to practice, develop, and apply the emotional learning initiated through the first two stages. Bear in mind that conduct and appreciation attributes are learned, so children need opportunities to practice and further develop and apply them. Individuals who examine their own learning of attributes will discover that practice gradually played a large part in their development. When completely developed, the attributes function in everyday living. When David decided to stay out of school because he was concerned about spreading germs in the classroom, he actually practiced and implemented this attribute/idea, and that practice strengthened his future response. Learning of attributes should continue until they function freely or without restraint.

In a certain elementary school, the custodian complained that the children left small bits of paper on the floor in the all-purpose room. He found it impossible to sweep them up. They could be removed only by the tedious labor of stooping and picking them up by hand. The custodian was an elderly gentleman, beloved by all the children. At dismissal that day, the scene can be described as follows:

> Principal: How many of you children have ever swept floors? [All hands go up.] What makes sweeping difficult?
>
> Jennifer (student): Sweeping under tables, chairs, the refrigerator, and all the other places that are hard to sweep under because of the furniture.
>
> Jose (student): Sweeping up anything on the floor that sticks really hard to the floor and is too small or flat to be budged. That means you have to stoop down and pick it up. It makes your back hurt from bending all the time, and you could break your fingernails.
>
> Principal: Yes, you know from experience. I'm sure that all of you realize what our custodian, Mr. Brock, does for us every day. Now, I'm going to let you in on a little secret. Today Mr. Brock told me that his hardest work during the day was sweeping this all-purpose room because there were so many bits of paper that stuck snuggly to the tile. He had to stoop many times each evening to pick them up, one by one. Couldn't we do something to help him?

The children saw the implication immediately, and from that moment they never left without picking up each bit of paper and other debris, and they did it voluntarily. In this illustration the first two stages of emotional learning occurred in a short period of time, but practice continued indefinitely. Practice instills the attribute so that it becomes part of living, and not until that fourth stage has been reached is the learning complete. Briefly, attributes must be practiced before they become part of living. Hearing, seeing, thinking, and feeling may initiate the practice, but complete learning of the attribute occurs when its implementation becomes part of living.

As evident in the elementary school example, however, children who practice an attribute must view its practice and repetition as self-satisfying. Further, continued practice is significantly influenced by others in the children's environment.

Ideal Environment for Attribute Development

A child's mind is enormously influenced by the impact of the environment. In reading the daily newspaper recently, I found the testimony of an eleven-year-old child, who'd told a judge that he would never get married in all of his life—never, never. You see, his parents were in court for divorce, and cruelty was the charge. The boy, living in this environment, was disgusted by the thought of marriage, embittered by one of life's most precious human relationships gone wrong. While this incident is only illustrative, it implies much for the teaching of attributes. Without the right environment, the attributes cannot effectively develop. What, then, is the right environment? In what kind of environment will the development of attributes flourish? Some aspects of an ideal environment are summarized below:

- The environment must provide the opportunity for observing the attributes or for seeing and hearing them being practiced. Children tend to practice those attributes that constantly impact their senses in the environment. While occasionally strong souls rise above the everyday environmental level, most souls do not exceed it.

    In an ideal school environment, one opportunity for children to learn or acquire attributes involves living with and learning from teachers—teachers with character, poise, balance, enthusiasm, and the highest personal integrity. No screen is required, no mechanical sound needs to be produced, and no electrical apparatus is needed. Teachers set the example for some of the most precious of all things to be learned. Teachers with pleasing and congenial attributes inspire youngsters to be happy and active. Humor cannot be learned from a sour and constantly disgruntled teacher, kindness from a cruel tyrant, broad-mindedness from a narrow-minded and biased teacher, or politeness from a rude and abrasive teacher. Whether children learn directly or indirectly, their learning will be influenced greatly by their teachers. What a real opportunity it is for pupils to live and work and practice within an environment created by teachers with genuine attributes. Teachers who demonstrate the attributes deemed valuable by our society play a key role in promoting the development of pupils' attributes.

In the area of attribute development, then, the teacher's impact is especially important. Character development basically results from human example and stimulation. If teachers fail to lead children to develop appreciations and positive attitudes through example and association with their students, they miss a most effective opportunity to promote health and development. Through interpersonal relationships with students, the bond between teacher and learner is strengthened. We cannot deceive children. They are keen observers and listeners. What the teacher demonstrates, children may learn and emulate.

If the scene of a film can produce significant changes in attitudes, is it not reasonable to believe that the pupils' constant observation of the real-life drama of a teacher in action will produce more profound changes in attributes? Is not the teacher's portrayal of sincerity, sympathy, patience, outlook on life, broad-mindedness, and scientific interest more effective than a film? Can one not learn by seeing a live demonstration as well as by watching a staged performance? The teacher's sociological influence must be recognized as an essential and vital component in the educational environment. Very little, if anything, is learned by accident; most often, even indirect learning is promoted by something that acts as a stimulus. Even elusive and subtle character development may be acquired indirectly but not accidentally. The genuineness of the teacher's strong personal attributes fosters within children each of the subtle developments that are commonly but erroneously said to be "caught and not taught."

❒ Teachers should arrange for the children's active participation. One tends to become what one does; one learns to appreciate what one practices appreciating. Often, people confess that they dislike a certain thing but then change completely after trying or experiencing it. Although there may be limits to learning attributes through active participation, no barrier should block children's attempts to reach the upper limit of learning them. In fact, opportunity for reaching the maximum limit should be provided. Real growth comes from stretching outward and upward to the maximum of one's potential. Teachers should make numerous arrangements for children's active participation in developing attributes linked to learning to live and learning how to make a living.

For example, experiencing music, art, recreational games, and drama facilitates a child's understanding, appreciation, and enjoyment of such activities. Appreciation attributes are essential to learning how to live, enjoying leisure time and recreation, and relating to others. The ability to appreciate and to enjoy may be influenced by the child's inherent capacities, but such ability is acquired nevertheless. It is desirable, therefore, and even urgent, that boys and girls be given every opportunity in school to experience, develop, and practice appreciation attributes desirable for living and making a living. We cannot expect these attributes to take care of themselves any more than we can expect health to take care of itself. A conscious effort must be made to gain anything worthwhile in life. In actuality, the dues must always be paid.

In addition to development of appreciation attributes, children do need to experience, develop, and practice conduct attributes, many of which are absolutely essential for learning to live and how to make a living. Experiencing and practicing politeness, neatness, punctuality, suspended judgment, self-control, independence, self-reliance, tolerance, honesty, and other conduct attributes influence children's ability to inculcate and demonstrate them in their own daily relationships and eventually in the work environment. Here again, the possessor must pay the price. These attributes do not take care of themselves. They are learned, and the teacher can significantly influence their inculcation in a properly designed learning environment.

❐ The ideal environment must be designed to facilitate the practice of appreciation and conduct attributes so that children's maximum inner transformation occurs. Consider the following:

- Give the children an active part in initiating and formulating the ways that call for demonstration of certain attributes. Adult enforcement produces conformity, but such conformity may be ephemeral. Children generally aim high; they are not bad or depraved by nature. Capitalizing upon children's best inclinations and leanings, a teacher can maintain momentum and guide children appropriately. What will be appreciated? What will the proper conduct be? The answers to these questions may be somewhat different, but the children's contributions should be sought and incorporated into the answers, as far as possible. If children feel that they have some part in the formulation of attributes, the attributes will be accepted and desirable in personal behavior/conduct. The child who brings a flower, picture, or anything to share with others to brighten the classroom becomes an active agent in the appreciation of the appearance and beauty of that room. The child who has some part in formulating a rule of good conduct on the playground will try to behave accordingly because that child is a stockholder in that rule.

- Make the practice lifelike, pleasant, and satisfying. Why should the appropriate conduct or appreciation of the higher things appear burdensome or possibly punitive? It should not. In many classrooms there has been too much dictating, scolding, threatening, forcing, and punishing when there should have been more guiding, leading, praising, suggesting, living, and learning. The principle of self-activity works as clearly in learning attributes as it does in any other type of learning. Since learning these attributes requires their practice, teachers should conduct activities that are pleasant and satisfying for the children.

◻ With regard to creating an ideal environment for attribute development, a fourth aspect involves encouraging constant application/implementation of appreciation and conduct attributes, not only in school but at home and elsewhere. Teachers need to maintain focus on application and implementation when the learning is complete. Of course, this stage is the final objective, subsequent to the first three stages that make this last stage possible.

Application Exercises

- ☐ Does understanding influence appreciation? Would pupils with very different levels of understanding poetry appreciate the same poems? Why?

- ☐ Are personal attributes learned more effectively indirectly or directly? Analyze your personal experiences in learning appreciation and conduct attributes.

- ☐ What poems do you like best? Why?

- ☐ How influential is the environment in encouraging the development of conduct attributes? Appreciation attributes? Do you think playgrounds and recreation areas are environments that could facilitate attribute development? Why?

- ☐ A boy who is not very honest was a contestant in a pumpkin-growing contest. He worked all summer to raise prize pumpkins, and the evening before the day of the judging, he walked about his large would-be prize winners and thought of the rewards he might win on the next day. While he was sleeping that night, someone stole his pumpkins. Finding the patch raided, the boy cried pitifully. He said between tears, "I never knew how bad a boy can feel when somebody steals from him." Will the boy likely be more careful of his own habit of taking from others after this experience? Why? Will such an experience encourage development of appropriate conduct attributes? Why?

PART 5

EMOTIONAL-TYPE LEARNING: IN LIGHT OF RECENT RESEARCH

Introduction

We now see much emphasis placed on social and emotional learning, as apparent in the literature and current research. It is critical, as Carline suggested when stressing the need to develop conduct and appreciation attributes, to inculcate social-emotional learning in today's classrooms. The attributes that Carline noted as essential for learning to live and how to make a living influence how individuals will conduct their lives and nurture relationships and how individuals will perform in the workplace. Proponents of social-emotional learning also stress the necessity of learning how to live and nurture relationships and the need for developing attributes that influence workplace success.

Greenberg et al. (2003) stated that the fundamental mission of K–12 in the twenty-first century is to ensure that all students become proficient in reading, writing, math, and science and demonstrate an understanding of history, literature, arts, foreign languages, and diverse cultures. Further, they indicated that "most educators, parents, students, and the public support a broader educational agenda that also involves enhancing students' social-emotional competence, character, health, and civic engagement" (466). They noted that while providing academic instruction, our schools must also focus on social-emotional skills in a way that will address causes of problem behavior. Many educators today hold that when schools address students' social-emotional skills, academic achievement increases, while problem behavior decreases (Elias et al. 1997).

Early Work

As early as 1983, Howard Gardner's *Frames of Mind: The Theory of Multiple Intelligences* was based on the notion that we are social and emotional beings. Gardner's influential model of multiple intelligences includes both interpersonal and intrapersonal intelligences. As Goleman (2011) indicated in an interview:

> When I wrote *Emotional Intelligence,* I was building on Howard Gardner's model of multiple intelligences. As I noted in the book, my model of emotional intelligence unpacks

what Gardner calls "intrapersonal" and "interpersonal" intelligences. In my theory, self-awareness and self-regulation are the intrapersonal abilities, and empathy and social skills the interpersonal. (www.danielgoleman.info/howard-gardner-multiple-intelligences)

Social and Emotional Learning (SEL)

Goleman (1995), in *Emotional Intelligence*, addressed factors involved when those of modest IQ excel and those with high IQ do not do as well. Such factors include self-control, persistence, and motivation, which are qualities of emotional intelligence. Emotional intelligence, at a fundamental level, refers to the abilities to recognize and regulate emotions in ourselves and others.

Goleman noted that the concept of emotional intelligence has been embraced by educators who have implemented programs in "social and emotional learning," or SEL. Elias et al. (1997) provided a framework for addressing the social-emotional needs of youngsters in our schools. In brief, they indicated that social-emotional learning can be viewed as the process of acquiring the skills to identify and manage emotions, establish and reach positive goals, appreciate others' perspectives, establish and maintain positive relationships, make responsible decisions, and effectively handle interpersonal situations. Such skills are necessary for success in the academic world / school, the workplace, and in life in general. Elias et al. noted specifically:

> Social and emotional competence is the ability to understand, manage, and express the social and emotional aspects of one's life in ways that enable the successful management of life tasks, such as learning, forming relationships, solving everyday problems, and adapting to the complex demands of growth and development. It includes self-awareness, control of impulsivity, working cooperatively, and caring about oneself and others. Social and emotional learning is the process through which children and adults develop the skills, attitudes, and values necessary to acquire social and emotional competence. (2)

Researchers generally agree on five key competencies for SEL, as noted by Durlak et al. (2011). These five competencies, which serve as a foundation for maintaining high-quality social relationships and for responding to life's challenges, are self-awareness, self-management, social awareness, relationship skills, and responsible decision making. Durlak et al. (2011) conducted a meta-analysis of 213 school-based, universal social and emotional learning programs involving over 270,000 K–12 students from rural, suburban, and urban areas, and they noted that SEL interventions decreased classroom misbehavior and aggression. Further, such interventions improved social and emotional skills and attitudes and improved academic performance. Such outcomes were demonstrated when teachers directly implemented effective SEL programs. The programs used sequenced learning activities so that skills were taught in a systematic way. Strategies included the use of active learning techniques, such as role play, and explicit and implicit description of SEL skills in the context of other learning activities.

Frequently associated with SEL is a significant reduction in students' conduct problems, classroom misbehavior and aggression, emotional distress and depression. SEL leads to significant improvement in students' social and emotional skills and their attitudes about themselves and their school, improved social and classroom behavior, and improved academic performance. A plethora of research demonstrates that helping children improve their self-awareness and confidence, increase their ability to manage disturbing emotions and impulses, and increase their empathy results in both improved behavior and in measurable academic achievement. Making this case was the meta-analysis of the 213 evaluation studies of SEL programs implemented in K–12 schools (Durlak et al. 2011). This analysis shows that students who demonstrate key SEL competencies increase success in school and later in life.

Keys to Implementation

In implementing SEL, as well as in providing instruction in academic areas, it is important that teachers interact with students in positive, caring ways and focus on student interests, problems, goal achievement, and social interactions, both inside and outside the classroom (Agne, Greenwood, and Miller 1994; Cotton 1996). In discussing a three-level approach to improving schools, Osher, Dwyer, and Jackson (2002) noted that when building a schoolwide foundation for all children, schools should do the following: "Support positive discipline, academic success, and mental and emotional wellness by providing a caring school environment to which all students, families and staff feel connected; teaching appropriate behaviors and problem-solving skills; and offering positive behavioral support and appropriate academic instruction" (7). In acknowledging the importance of using effective support to build positive relationships, the Canters (2002) indicated, "Sometimes it takes more than praise or setting limits to let kids know that you care. It takes being interested in them" (219).

Payton et al. (2008) conducted large-scale reviews of research on the impact of SEL programs on elementary and middle school students. They found that those interventions determined to be effective for skills training in schools included a sequenced, organized set of activities that develop skills sequentially and that use different forms of active learning, such as role play and behavioral rehearsal with feedback. They noted that those interventions found to be effective devote focused and adequate time to developing identified social and emotional skills. In short, Payton et al. (2008) labeled four evidence-based training practices as SAFE:

- ❐ **Se**quenced instruction or coordinated instructional steps
- ❐ **A**ctive learning strategies
- ❐ **F**ocus on developing social-emotional skills
- ❐ **E**xplicit targeting or teaching of specific skills (6–7)

Such practices were found to significantly improve outcomes.

Common Core State Standards

With the more recent emphasis on the Common Core State Standards (CCSS), adopted in many of our nation's schools, Zakrzewski (2014) raised the question about appropriate integration of social-emotional learning into the Common Core and how to align the CCSS within the framework of social-emotional learning outcomes. In perusing the CCSS, however, Zakrzewski noted that social-emotional skills are implicitly embedded in the standards even though the teachers may not be aware of their inclusion. Also, she indicated that for students to successfully meet the standards, they must possess social-emotional skills, and deliberate teaching of these skills is necessary. For example, as Zakrzewski indicated, many CCSS language arts standards offer teachers the opportunity to incorporate mini-lessons on emotions, communication, relationships, and other social-emotional skills directly into the language arts curriculum. In the *California Common Core State Standards: English Language Arts and Literacy in History / Social Studies, Science, and Technical Subjects (2013)*, Standard RL 3.3 reads, "Describe characters in a story, (e.g., their traits, motivations, or feelings) and explain how their actions contribute to the sequence of events" (12).

Zakrzewski (2014) identified SEL skills related to Standard RL 3.3. She indicated, "Corresponding SEL skills of self-awareness, social awareness, and responsible decision-making skills: label and recognize own and others' emotions; analyze emotions and how they affect others; evaluate others' emotional reactions; and reflect on how current choices affect one's future" (3).

Zakrzewski emphasized, however, that no CCSS or SEL program can replace a teacher's excitement and dedication to what he or she is teaching. She indicated that truly great teachers care for their students and lead them to see many wonders around them. Further, she suggested that such teachers help their students identify their purpose in life and the world. And Vega (2012) pointed out that both teachers and administrators must practice SEL competencies in order to teach them effectively.

Preparation for the Workplace

In addition to helping students meet CCSS, teachers implement SEL as a means to provide a caring, warm learning environment for helping students prepare for the workplace. School goals should include workplace preparation in an environment that instills social and emotional skills (Cotton 1995). The goal is to ensure that students develop learning strategies and creative thinking skills, both of which are required in the modern workplace. Further, emphasis should be placed on developing social-emotional skills that are needed for handling various roles in society and for completing routine tasks, such as interacting successfully with others in the workplace (Elias 2006).

Collaborative for Academic, Social, and Emotional Learning (CASEL)

Based on a review of the evidence, the Collaborative for Academic, Social and Emotional Learning (CASEL) (2003) has suggested that SEL interventions and skill development should be taught within a supportive learning environment and contribute to its enhancement. Such interventions will lead to positive child development and greater achievement and engagement in school (Zins et al., eds. 2004).

According to the results of in-depth research, numerous SEL programs are available for broad implementation in today's schools. On CASEL's website (www.CASEL.org/guide/programs), a number of examples are described, including the following:

- PATHS (Promoting Alternative Thinking Strategies) includes 40-52 lessons per grade for PreK-6 students. This program focuses on conflict resolution, empathy, and responsible decision making. Implementation results in improved academic performance, increased positive social behavior, reduced conduct problems, and reduced emotional distress (53).
- 4 R's (reading, writing, respect, and resolution) includes explicit skills instruction provided over thirty-five weeks, one lesson per week, for PreK-8 students. Implementation results in improved academic performance for students at behavioral risk, increased positive social behavior, and reduced conduct problems and emotional distress (43).
- Second Step provides explicit skills instruction in areas including learning, empathy, emotion management, friendship skills, and problem solving. Lessons are implemented over 22–28 weeks per year for PreK-8 students (60).

The *2013 CASEL Guide: Effective Social and Emotional Learning Programs, Pre-School, Elementary School Edition* provides an overview of social and emotional learning; describes review methods; provides the framework for evaluating the quality of available SEL programs; employs the framework for identifying select CASEL programs for use in the classroom; and summarizes future directions (4). CASEL, cofounded by Daniel Goleman, is dedicated to advancing the science and practice of school-based social and emotional learning. As noted on CASEL's website, CASEL's mission is to make social and emotional learning an integral part of education from preschool through high school.

It is clear that a plethora of research supports SEL and the role of compassionate, caring teachers who focus on the interests and well-being of their students. Such research expands upon Carline's recommendations and reinforces his suggestions for teachers working with students in the classroom to develop conduct and appreciation attributes. While SEL literature was not available when he prepared his material used herein, the ideas that he advanced were most similar. In this regard, he was truly ahead of his time, and his work is best described as timeless wisdom.

References for Part 5—Emotional-Type Learning

Agne, K., G. E. Greenwood, and L. D. Miller. 1994. "Relationships between Teacher Belief Systems and Teacher Effectiveness." *Journal of Research and Development in Education* 27, no. 3: 141–152.

Bourdillon, F. W. 1873. "The Night Has a Thousand Eyes." *The Spectator* 13.

California Common Core State Standards: English Language Arts and Literature in in History/Social Studies, Science, and Technical Subjects. 2013. Sacramento, CA: California Department of Education.

Canter, L., and M. Canter. 2002. *Assertive Discipline: Positive Behavior Management for Today's Classroom.* Bloomington, IN: Solution Tree Press.

Collaborative for Academic, Social, and Emotional Learning (CASEL). 2003. *Safe and Sound: An Educational Leader's Guide to Evidence-Based Social and Emotional Learning (SEL) Programs.* Chicago, IL: Author.

Collaborative for Academic, Social, and Emotional Learning (CASEL). 2012. *2013 CASEL Guide: Effective Social and Emotional Learning Programs—Preschool and Elementary School Edition.* Chicago, IL: Author.

Cotton, K. 1995. "Effective Schooling Practices: A Research Synthesis—1995 Update." Northwest Regional Educational Laboratory. www.nwrel.org/scpd/esp/esp95.html.

Cotton, K. 1996. "School Size, School Climate, and Student Performance." Northwest Regional Educational Laboratory. School Improvement Research Series. http://www.nwrel.org/scpd/sirs/10/c020.html.

Durlak, J. A., R. P. Weissberg, A. B. Dymnicki, R. D. Taylor, and K. B. Schellinger. 2011. "The Impact of Enhancing Students' Social and Emotional Learning: A Meta-analysis of School-Based Universal Interventions." *Child Development* 82, no. 1: 405–432.

Elias, M. J., J. E. Zins, R. P. Weissberg, K. S. Frey, M. T. Greenberg, N. M. Haynes, R. Kessler, M. E. Schwab-Stone, and T. P. Shriver. 1997. *Promoting Social and Emotional Learning: Guidelines for Educators.* Alexandria, VA: Association for Supervision and Curriculum Development (ASCD).

Elias, M. J. 2006. "The Connection between Academic and Social-Emotional Learning." In *The Educator's Guide to Emotional Intelligence and Academic Achievement*, edited by M. J. Elias and H. Arnold, 4–14. Thousand Oaks, CA: Corwin Press.

Gardner, H. 1983. *Frames of Mind: The Theory of Multiple Intelligences.* New York, NY: Basic Books.

Goleman, D. 1995. *Emotional Intelligence: Why It Can Matter More than IQ.* New York: Bantam Books.

Goleman, D. 2011. "Question and Answer." www.danielgoleman.info/howard-gardner-multiple-intelligences.

Greenberg, M. T., R. P. Weissberg, M. Utne-O'Brien, J. Zins, L. Fredericks, H. Resnik, and M. J. Elias. 2003. "Enhancing School-Based Prevention and Youth Development through Coordinated Social, Emotional, and Academic Learning." *American Psychologist* 58, no. 6/7: 466–474.

Osher, D., K. Dwyer, and S. Jackson. 2002. "Safe, Supportive, and Successful Schools: Step by Step." Rockville, MD: US Department of Health and Human Services, Substance Abuse and Mental Health Services Administration. Center for Mental Health Services.

Payton, J., R. P. Weissberg, J. A. Durlak, A. B. Dymnicki, R. D. Taylor, K. B. Schellinger, and M. Pachan. 2008. "The Positive Impact of Social and Emotional Learning for Kindergarten to Eighth-Grade Students: Findings from Three Scientific Reviews." Chicago, IL: Collaborative for Academic, Social and Emotional Learning.

Vega, V. 2012. "Social and Emotional Learning Research Review: Avoiding Pitfalls." *Eutopia* (November). San Rafael, CA: George Lucas Educational Foundation.

Zakrzewski, V. 2014. "How to Integrate Social-Emotional Learning into the Common Core." *Greater Good: The Science of the Meaningful Life* (January). Greater Good Science Center Newsletter. University of California, Berkeley.

Zins, J. E., R. P. Weissberg, M. C. Wang, and H. J. Walberg, eds. 2004. *Building Academic Success on Social and Emotional Learning: What Does the Research Say?* New York, NY: Teachers College Press.

CPSIA information can be obtained
at www.ICGtesting.com
Printed in the USA
LVHW100030231122
733811LV00001B/68